P9-DWH-567

Hobbyist Guide
To
Marine Fish & Invertebrates

Aquarium Digest International
Collector's Edition

Hobbyist Guide To Marine Fish & Invertebrates

Dr. Chris Andrews

Tetra-Press
Tetra Werke Dr. rer nat. Ulrich Baensch GmbH
P.O. Box 1580, D-4520 Melle, Germany

1 st edition 1-10.000, 1991
Printed in Spain by Egedsa
DL. B-23245-91
Distributed in U.S.A. by
Tetra Sales (Division of Warner-Lambert)
Morris Plains, N.J. 07950
Distributed in UK by Tetra Sales, Lambert Court,
Chestnut Avenue, Eastleigh Hampshire 505 3ZQ
WL-Code: 16582

ISBN 3-89356-133-1

CONTENTS

Editorial Comments

Dr. Chris Andrews

In this special combined re-issue of the *Aquarium Digest* we deal with the increasingly popular subject of marine aquarium keeping - both fish and invertebrates. A number of European aquarists offer their opinions on a range of current topics, and (as always) there is often more than one solution to any given problem. Observant readers will also notice some discrepancies with regard to the scientific nomenclature of certain species, although we have tried to use the scientific names in most common usage on both sides of the Atlantic.

Reasonably priced (and healthy) fish and invertebrates are now available, and the standard of the equipment for the marine hobbyist means that setting up a marine tank need be no more complex (and the losses no greater) than when setting up a large tropical freshwater aquarium.

Where the difference really lies is with the approach of the hobbyist. To begin with the setting up and establishment of a marine tank cannot be rushed, and the "text book" recommendations concerning initial stocking levels (with hardy fish) must be adhered to. Furthermore, and as is indicated by several authors in this *Aquarium Digest*, marine fish and invertebrates come from a stable environment, which means that the hobbyist has to not only create the correct tank conditions, but then proceed to keep them stable. This means diligent and regular tank maintenance and hence marine aquarium keeping is not for the lazy aquarist!

In this issue we have tried to touch on most of the popular aspects of marine aquarium keeping, and provide an insight into the natural environment of the fishes and invertebrates. Your local marine specialist shop should be able to offer you a number of useful guides or texts on marine aquaria, and there are also a number of marine aquarium clubs in North America and the British Isles. Details of these clubs should be available from the monthly hobbyist magazines.

If you are already a marine hobbyist, I am sure you will find the observations of fellow hobbyists contained in this magazine of great interest. If you are a newcomer, or still debating whether or not to set-up a marine tank, let the information in the following pages guide you through the early stages - and onto the challenges of keeping marine corals and breeding coral fishes.

Coral reef fish abound beneath these sparkling clear waters.

Amongst the factors of special relevance to would be marine invertebrate specialists are *aquarium water depth* and *fish density*. Many hobbyists find it easier to adequately illuminate, filter, maintain and feed relatively small invertebrates aquaria (perhaps no more than 50 gallons), and that for adequate illumination a water depth of (say) 18-24 inches should be looked upon as a maximum. Similarly, invertebrates do not seem to thrive in tanks which contain large numbers of even quite inoffensive fish.

Of all marine invertebrates currently offered by dealers, it is the hard stony reef building corals that are amongst the most difficult to maintain in the home aquarium for longer than a few months. Therefore, until the needs of these delicate, beautiful and environmentally very important creatures are better understood, and more easily provided in the home aquarium, we have deliberately featured other (soft) corals in this magazine, as well as anemones, crabs, shrimps, sea slugs, gorgonians, sea stars,....!

Best wishes

Dr. Chris Andrews

Starting a tropical marine aquarium

Just a few years ago marine fishkeeping was looked upon as more of a dream than a reality. However, with recent advances in equipment, salt mixes and suitable foods for use in the marine aquarium, along with the greater availability of healthy stock, marine fishkeeping is no longer an activity for just the advanced hobbyist. In fact, anyone can now maintain a beautiful selection of marine fish and invertebrates in the home aquarium.

Anyone intending to set up a marine tank is advised to read through one or two books on the subject, and to get in contact with other local marine hobbyists. With some background information, it is then a good idea to seek out a reliable local dealer and to go along and discuss your requirements with him. He should be only too willing to help you plan your venture into the marine hobby.

The *Marine Aquarist Manual* should be available from your local *Tetra* stockist, and is an excellent introduction to marine fishkeeping. The following hints may also prove useful.

The tank size

Marine fishes are accustomed to living in one of the most stable environments in the world - the coral reef. The larger the tank, the slower are any changes in water quality which take place, and the more stable are the tank conditions. So the minimum recommended tank size is about 25 U.S. gallons, although larger tanks are preferable. Filled aquaria are heavy - a 3 foot long setup tank may weigh 200-300 pounds, so it will need a firm even base or stand.

Water quality

Sea water is very complex and is composed of many elements, some only present in trace amounts (see page 122). The best aquarium water is not natural sea water, due to the fact that it may contain dangerous pollutants or harmful bacteria and parasites. Today a number of synthetic, high quality salt mixes are available, enabling aquarists to produce perfect sea water for aquarium use. Ask your local aquarium shop for details.

Made up following the manufacturers instructions, a good salt mix should result in the correct specific gravity and pH conditions in the aquarium (see below).

Specific gravity

Careful control of the salt content (specific gravity) of the water is most important. The internal salt balance in the body of marine organisms is sensitive to water conditions, and if this balance is upset, serious harm may result. At tropical sea water temperatures, the specific

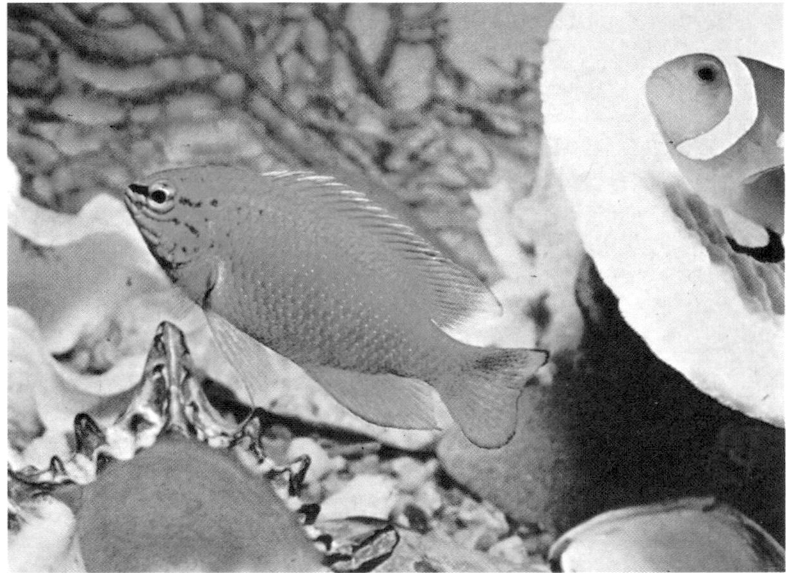

The blue damsel (Chrysiptera cyanea) is an attractive fish, and hardy enough for beginners tank. *Photo: B. Kahl*

gravity should measure between 1.020 and 1.022, and can be easily measured using an aquarium hydrometer (the latter of which should be calibrated for use at tropical aquarium temperatures). The specific gravity can be decreased by adding freshwater, or increased by adding salt.

pH

The ideal pH for a marine aquarium is 8.0 to 8.3, as the open oceans of the world are usually slightly to moderately alkaline. pH values slightly above this range are less dangerous than those below. Water with a pH below 8.0 is extremely harmful to marine fishes, and in such an event an immediate water change is necessary. There is a tendency for the pH to fall (become more acid) in the marine aquarium, and hence there is a need to regularly measure the pH using a reliable test kit. Regular partial water changes, along with the occasional use of a buffer solution (available from aquarium shops) should keep the pH within the desired range.

Water temperature

The temperature of the water on coral reefs around the world normally ranges between 21 and 28 °C, but is usually stable within a narrow range at each locality. A temperature of around 25° C (78 or 79° F) is recommended for marine tanks, and it is important to keep the temperature constant within a degree or so.

Ammonia and nitrite

Vital to the successful maintenance of a marine aquarium is a basic understanding of the principles of biological filtration - or the nitrogen cycle.

The main nitrogenous waste product of fish is ammonia, and in alkaline water like sea water ammonia is particularly toxic - to both fishes and invertebrates. In the aquarium, however, helpful bacteria in the undergravel filter (or power filter) use ammonia as a source of food and convert it to less toxic nitrate via nitrite (the latter of which is also poisonous to marine organisms). Nitrate is less toxic, and usually kept at a safe level by regular, partial water changes.

Bacteria known as *Nitrosomonas* convert ammonia to nitrite, and then *Nitrobacter* bacteria convert the nitrite to nitrate. In new tanks, neither of these two bacteria exist in any numbers, and consequently there is a characteristic rise in ammonia and nitrite as they become established. Once the biological filter has been running for about four weeks, the ammonia and nitrite levels should have subsided to safe levels. This means that for the first month or six weeks only pollution tolerant fish such as damsels can be kept. Then, once the ammonia and nitrite levels (as indicated by a *Tetra* test kit) have declined, other more sensitive fish

The royal Gramma (Gramma loreto) is suitable for the marine community aquarium. Photo: K. Paysan

The lesson surgeon (Zebrasoma flavescens) and the red- tailed surgeon (Acanthurus achilles) are hardy alternative inmates for the home aquarium.
Photo: H. Ruffus

can be kept. To keep ammonia and nitrite at safe levels, the tank must not be overstocked or overfed and the filter must be left running 24 hours a day and regularly serviced. Regular water quality monitoring will ensure that ammonia and nitrite levels do not exceed safe limits.

Filtration and aeration

A common and quite efficient method of filtration of a marine aquarium is the undergravel filter. Such a filter, driven by an uplift from an air pump or by a power filter, acts both mechanically, by physically trapping suspended debris in the filter bed, and biologically, by breaking down waste products from the fish and uneaten food via the nitrogen cycle. The filter bed in a marine tank should consist of a layer of washed cockleshell (to maintain an alkaline pH), on top of which is placed a layer of unwashed coral sand (the biological filter). The two can be separated using a gravel tidy. Use 10 pounds of cockleshell and 10 pounds of coral sand per square foot of tank bottom.

Undergravel filters must be regularly cleaned using a siphon tube to 'hoover' the tank floor thus preventing a buildup of unwanted debris. 'Gravel washers' are also available for in tank use.
An outside power filter supplements the action of the biological filter. Filter materials include foam, nylon wool and activated carbon.
Marine fishes and invertebrates require well aerated water, and if the supply of aerated water through the filter bed is turned off for long periods, the helpful filter bacteria will also die, with consequent water quality problems for the tank livestock.
Therefore, not only must marine aquaria be continuously well aerated, but the filters must be left running continuously (with only short breaks for cleaning, etc.).

Lighting

Provide about 100 watts of cool white fluorescent lighting for every 60 U.S. gallons of water. Some invertebrates may need more than this though.

The decorations

All decorative items must be inert and not give off dangerous chemicals. Corals and shells are normally chosen for the marine tank and these days most coral sold for aquarium use is already cleaned and cured. When buying coral, be sure to select those pieces which appear clean as well as attractive.

Marine plants

There is not a great variety of aquatic plants available to the marine aquarist. Many of the 'plants' that are kept in the marine aquarium disintegrate and quickly rot, thereby polluting the tank water. The majority of marine hobbyists, advanced as well as beginners, tend to avoid live plants and settle for the life-like plastic plants which closely resemble living species of marine algae, or coral decorations. However, the best kind of 'plant' for a tropical marine aquarium is *Caulerpa,* a bright green alga which has the appearance of a higher plant.

Stocking

Compatibility can be a problem in marine tanks, so decide early on if you want a fish only, invertebrate only, or mixed tank, and discuss suitable tank inmates with your local dealer. After the ammonia-nitrite has declined to a negligible level, gradually increase the stock to a maximum of one inch of fish per 5 U.S. gallons of water over six months. After twelve months this may be increased to one inch of fish per 2.5 U.S. gallons. Provide plenty of rock refuges for the fishes.

Feeding

Tetra flaked, tablet and freeze-dried foods are an ideal diet for most marine fish. Feed 2-3 times per day, with only as much as is consumed in a few minutes. Feed invertebrates twice a week; anemones and most

crustaceans on tablet or gamma-irradiated frozen foods, filter-feeders on a liquid invertebrate food. Vitamin and trace element supplements are also available (see later).

Water changes

A key factor in maintaining good water quality for marine life is in regularly checking, and partially changing, the water. It is necessary to replace trace and other elements removed by the inhabitants and to keep the salts in proper balance. Every 2-4 weeks check the specific gravity, pH and nitrite or ammonia content of the water. Then change 20-25 % of the tank volume and replace with fresh salt water at the correct specific gravity and temperature. The tank water can be removed via a siphon tube, along with any debris which has accumulated on the tank floor.

Selecting healthy fishes

Only healthy, active fishes should be purchased and very recently imported or sickly individuals should be avoided. Danger signs include the fish not eating properly, being constantly chased by other tank inmates with an inability to protect its home ground or territory, and rapid gill movements or 'scratching' against rocks or the gravel. Physical appearance is also important. Colours should be bright, the skin clear and free from parasites. A thin fish is a sick fish. Prior to a purchase, check the head region for signs of emaciation. If the head appears sunken in at the sides, the fish is not in good health.

◄ Small wrasse are good innates for the aquarium when young

Acclimating the fishes

Introducing a fish into an aquarium can be a traumatic experience - for both aquarist and fish! The fish is transferred from one environment to another, and these may differ physically and chemically. Check the conditions of the dealer's tank and (if necessary) make adjustments to your own. Floating the plastic bag containing the new fish within the aquarium is an acceptable method, but it is best to pour the bag contents into a jug and gradually add small amounts of aquarium water over a period of time, eventually allowing the fish to be released into the aquarium. To avoid squabbles in the tank following the introduction of an new fish, it is sometimes a good idea to rearrange the rocks and coral in the tank just before releasing the new fish, and to then leave the tank lights off for 12-24 hours.

Diseases

Marine organisms, just like any others, are subject to diseases. Incorrect tank care, especially poor water quality and overcrowding, will increase the susceptibility of most marine fish to disease. However, proper tank care is not the only factor in preventing disease outbreaks in the aquarium. Unless you are sure of the health status of new stock, all new fish and invertebrates should be quarantined in a separate tank for at least two weeks. Would-be marine hobbyists should note that some disease treatments are toxic to marine invertebrates or the helpful bacteria in the filter. Consequently only 'safe' remedies should be used in a set-up marine tank, especially if invertebrates are present.

by H. Leitz

Fishes for the Marine Aquarium

Once a marine tank is set up, the temptation to run to the nearest aquarium shop and buy the most colorful and bizarre fishes is hard to overcome. Selection of marine fishes based on their brilliant colors or unusual shapes is a mistake which the novice hobbyist must learn to avoid. The success of the aquarium will depend in large part on the proper selection and acclimation of its inhabitants. There are four basic steps which should be followed. These are (1) selecting the proper types of fish, (2) selecting the correct number of fish, (3) selecting healthy fish, and (4) properly acclimating the fish to be home aquarium. The latter three points have been discussed in the previous article.

Which Fish Are Best

A wide variety of marine fishes are offered for sale. Knowing which types are easy or difficult to maintain, and which types are suitable for the community tank is important. Certain groups of coral reef fishes should not be purchased by the novice. They require special diets or living conditions which the inexperienced hobbyist may not know how to provide. Nothing is more discouraging than to lose valuable fishes within a few days of their purchase. Exotic butterflies (chaetodons) and angels (pomacanthids) are highly prized for their rarity and fantastic colors, but many of these fish are difficult to maintain. The following list contains 14 families of marine fish. From among these groups, 90% of the fish in the aquarium hobby are to be found. The selection of these particular fishes is based on their popularity, their level of maintenance requirements, and their suitability for life in a community tank. Each family is

Pomacanthus imperator, an exceptionally beautiful coral reel fish, suited to a large aquarium only .
Photo: B. Kahl

Centropyge flavissimus, a very popular dwarf anglefish. *Photo: K. Paysan*

given a number. The compatibility of one group with another can be determined by reading the numbers following each group. This list is by no means complete and much additional information can be obtained from good reference books, and by asking the advice of dealers handling marine fishes.

1. Family Blennidae-Blennies. Most species compatible with 2, 3, 4, 5, 6, 7, 9, 10, 12.
2. Family Gobiidae-Gobies. Most species compatible with 1, 3, 4, 5, 6, 7, 9, 10, 12.
3. Family Pomacentridae-Damsels. Most species compatible with 1, 2, 4, 5, 6, 7, 10, 11.
4. Family Chaetodontidae-Butterflies. Many species of butterflies are difficult to maintain. Those recommended for the beginner include *C. auriga, C. lunula, C. semilarvatus, Heniochus varius,* and *H. acuminatus.* These species are compatible with 1, 2, 3, 5, 6, 7, 9, 10, 11, 12, 13, 14.
5. Family Pomacanthidae-Angels. Many species of angels are difficult to maintain. Those recommended for the beginner include *P. imperator, P. maculosus, Holacanthus ciliaris,* and *P. arcuatus.* These species are compatible with 1, 2, 3, 4, 6, 7,11.

6. Family Labridae-Wrasses. Smaller specimens of most species are compatiblewith l, 2, 3, 4, 5, 7, 8, 9, 10, 11,1 2.
7. Family Acanthuridae-Tangs. Most species are compatible with 1, 2, 3, 4, 5, 6, 8, 9, 10, 11, 13, 14.
8. Family Balistidae - Triggerfish. Smaller specimens of most species are compatible with 6, 7, 11, 13, 14.
9. Family Monacanthidae-Filefish. Most species are compatible with 1, 2, 4, 6, 7, 10, 11, 13, 14.
10. Family Platacidae-Batfish. The singe species *P. orbicularis*. It is compatiblewith 1, 2, 3, 4, 6, 7, 9, 11 and 12.
11. Family Ostraciontidae-Trunkfish. Cowfish, and Boxfish. Smaller specimens of most species are compatible with 3, 4, 5, 6, 7, 8, 9,10, 13, 14.
12. Family Apogonidae-Cardinal Fish. Most species are compatible with 1, 2, 4, 6, 10.
13. Family Serranidae - Groupers. Smaller specimens of most species are compatible with 4, 7, 8, 9, 11.
14. Familiy Lutianidae - Snappers. Smaller specimens of most species are compatible with 4, 7, 8, 9, 11.

by C. Smith

Diving in the Californian kelp beds

As a skin diver who has been spoilt by the most beautiful underwater habitats of the Indo-Pacific and Atlantic Oceans, I seized the opportunity, while visiting friends in San Diego, USA, to investigate the Pacific fauna and flora off the coast of California with my camera. All I had heard beforehand was that the water in this area was relatively cold and that there were no corals, but that this was made up for by the unique flora of the forests of seaweed, which provided the skin diver on the lookout for possible photos with new and exciting impressions. And let me say right away-I was not disappointed!

Skin diving on the coast of California is run on very professional lines, and that has a lot of advantages for the tourist, since here skin diving with sensible safety precautions must be described as a sport that is available to everyone. This is certainly not the case in many other countries. In Europe, for example, where can you receive instruction in skin diving at school or university? In California the often time-consu-

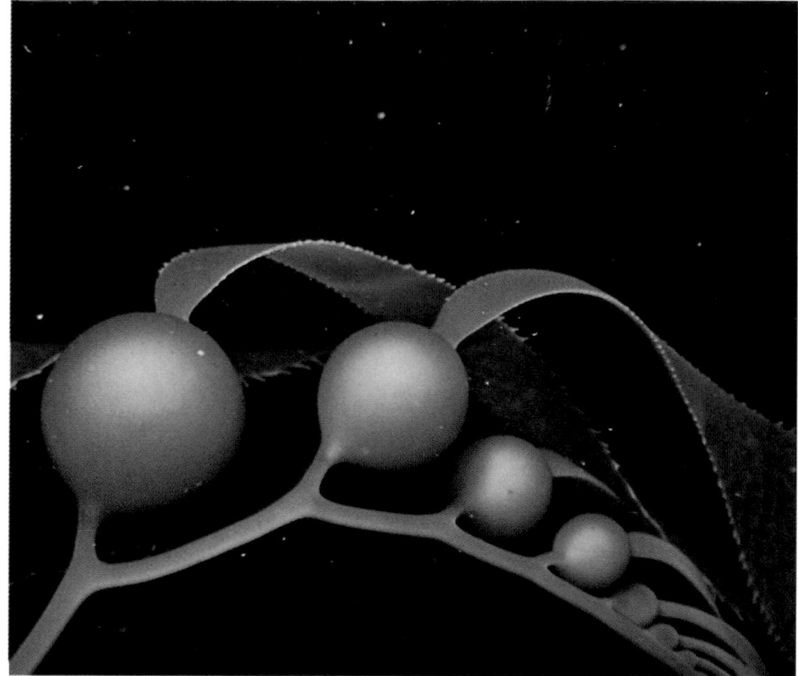

Californian kelp in close-up. *Photo: H. Debelius*

ming search for diving bases and equipment is unnecessary; here you can easily find a chance to take part in one of the regular, organised diving expeditions. Thus at at 11 o'clock at night, in the port in San Diego, I went aboard the *Bottom Scratcher*, a boat fully equipped for diving expeditions, which was to arrive at the off-shore island of San Clemente the next morning.

As I had been told before, the water directly off the coast was cloudy at this time of year (in February) because of the rough sea, so that it would have been senseless to have gone diving with my camera in the inshore areas. But the water around the off-shore island was as smooth as a mill pond and visibility was often more than 70 feet. I could hardly wait to put on my diving suit after anchoring at 7 o'clock in the morning. As it happened, my diving partner was also an aquarist, and in a conversation during the trip he had been able to give me some important tips on this underwater world which was completely new to me.

On my first look around in the rocks at a depth of 25 feet, I realised at once that I had never before seen an underwater habitat whose appearence was formed so extensively by one plant: the kelp, *Macrocystis*

A juvenile Garibaldi fish. The species is a relative of the commonly kept damsel fishes
Photo: H. Debelius

pyrifera, a seaweed-like plant which roots itself to rocky ground and pushes up to the water surface. Because of its length and abundance, it covered the whole area and the various shades of green made a splendid contrast to the deep blue water. In spite of its dependence on light, I have sometimes seen it at depths below 30 feet; I was fascinated by the jungle-like flora. It should also be mentioned that kelp is used commercially and is harvested on the Californian coast by special ships. One of its uses is, believe it or not, in dried food for aquarium fishes!

This 'jungle' was traversed by an eyecatching fish, the orange Garibaldi, *Hypsypops rubicunda* It is possibly the only fish which is protected on the West Coast of the USA, because it occurs only there, and on account of its appearance it would certainly soon be exterminated by over-collection. I was completely unacquainted with it as an adult fish, although I had previously seen photographs of juvenile Garibaldis. Fully grown it was not immediately recognisable to me as a representative of the Pomacentridae (damsels); at least I had never before seen a fish in this family which grows to a length of 8 inches.

The juvenile fish, which has blue spots on its red-orange body, is easier to classify among the Poma-

Garibaldi fish feed from the hand, almost as if they know the divers mean them no harm. *Photo: H. Debelius*

Catalina goby against rocky background. *Photo: H. Debelius*

centridae. Whereas the young fish were scurrying timidly to and fro among the roots of the kelp near to the bottom, the adults were swimming boldly in front of the diver in the open water. Apparently the reason for this is that San Clemente is frequently visited by divers and the fish are used to people. My diving partner soon showed me an example of their tameness using a sea urchin. As soon as he had cut open the sea urchin and put out his hand, it was immediately surrounded by several fully grown Garibaldis which ate from his fingers. They did not let themselves be distracted by divers taking pictures. Unlike the timid inhabitants of the kelp landscape, the adult Garibaldis continued to follow us while we went off in search of tasty abalone mussels.

The juvenile Garibaldi is undoubtedly a very attractive fish, and would be an ideal inmate for the home aquarium, where its colour combination of azure blue spots on a red-orange background would be especially striking. However careful control of fishing in this region help conserve this beautiful fish.

A member of our party had designed a piece of apparatus for catching fish. This was made out of a clear plastic suction tube with plunger, and with practice it was possible to quickly and safely catch a variety of small fishes as they swam in and out of the kelp. Some Catalina gobies, and even one or two Garibaldi fish, were caught, but our boat skipper made sure that these were all returned safely to the sea. In the wild, by the way, Garibaldi fish live in water

A haunting picture through the kelp beds. *Photo: H. Debelius*

with a maximum temperature of about 16 °C (61 °F). However, I have seen them in display aquaria where they can be slowly acclimated to higher temperatures (say 21 °C or 70 °F), and where their growth and maturation was quite fast.

The above mentioned Catalina goby, *Lythrypnus dalli, is* a much sought after aquarium fish from California's coastline. It belongs to the family Gobiidae and, with its contrasting colours, does not grow longer than 2 inches. The story of its discovery is interesting. It was first described in 1890, when a specimen of this species was caught in a net in the port of the town of Catalina at a depth of 230 feet. In the years that followed this fish was never caught again, and it was thus assumed that it was very rare and lived only in very deep water. At the end of the 'thirties', the American ichthyologist Vernon Brock heard about the invention of the aqua-lung, and began using this apparatus to obtain information about life in the ocean depths. In 1933 he then wrote that the Catalina goby was one of the commonest fish occuring off the Californian coast. It is found below a depth of 20 feet, but lives hidden in cavities and crevices. I can confirm Brock's findings because I too saw these fish quite frequently. However, they are more timid than the Garibaldis, and for this reason, and because of their smallness, they are difficult to photograph. As far as I know, they have only been occasionally exported to Europe over the last few years.

I was amazed at the large number of rockfish *(Sebastes)* which we saw, and up to now I understand that over 55 species have been identified from Californian waters. The common orange colouration of the fish I saw in California was something which I had not seen in rockfish from other areas.

There are very many invertebrates in the sea off the Californian coast. Of the many species of anemones, the red-white beadlet anemone was particularly eye-catching, the intensity of its colours coming out to the full in the camera flash. All the divers were equally captivated by the magnificent colours of the night snails, and I saw many new colour combinations, which once again evoked in me deep admiration for nature's variety.

In the short time I had for my holiday, and because of the infrequency of the diving expeditions, I could not, of course, form a complete picture of the Californian-Pacific environment. Nonetheless, I did also visit two excellent public aquaria while I was in the area. The Scripps Aquarium (San Diego) and the Steinhart Aquarium (San Francisco) provided a fitting end to my holiday, a trip that I will remember for some time to come.

by Helmut Debelius

Underwater Butterflies

Among the most colorful denizens of the tropical seas are the butterfly fishes. Found in tropical waters throughout the world, the Chaetodontidae family lives primarily in the shallow regions around the coral reefs. The strongly compressed, disclike shape and extended snout are clear identifying characteristics of these fishes. Butterfly fishes have small mouths with rows of tiny, brushlike teeth lining the jaws. Their brilliant colors and markings act as a type of camouflage for protection among the dazzling coral reefs, and many species have a false „eye" at the rear of the body, further adding to their disguise. Unlike their close relatives the marine angel fishes, with which they are sometimes confused, butterfly fishes have compact fins which are neither greatly extended nor delicate and flowing. Scales are relatively large and many extend over the bases of their fins. Great differences in shape and color between young and mature butterfly fishes are quite common. Some species actually undergo a unique 'Tholichthys" larval stage in which they look like a thorny burr. This spiny appearance fades early in development. Fully grown butterfly fishes range in length from

An active occasionally aggresive marine species, the threadfin butterfly fish (Chaetodon auriga) is generally hardy and easy to care for. It is native to the Indo-Pacific and the Red Sea and grows to 7 inchs in aquaria

Photo: B. Kahl

The red-striped butterfly fish (Chaetodon lunula) is found in shallow waters of the Indo-Pacific region. An enthusiastic feeder, this fish takes brine shrimp and Tubifex eagerly. Its maximum length is abaout 8 inches. Here C. lunula is shown in its yellow color phase. *Photo: A. van den Nieuwenhuizen*

Native to tropical waters from Red Sea to Indonesia, the pearlscale butterfly fish (Chaetodon chrysurus) is one of the most attractive species in the Chaetodon family. This fish is generally peacefull and does not require a great deal of care in the marine aquarium. Its length is 6 inches.
Photo: H. Baensch

Chaetodon collare is native to the Red Sea, and is a relatively delicate butterfly fish. *Photo: H.Baensch*

4-12 inches. In setting up a tank for butterfly fishes, the hobbyist should remember that they are lively, active swimmers and require plenty of room. A minimum tank length for an aquarium containing a small group of these fishes would be about 30 inches. Butterfly fishes are somewhat timid, and numerous hiding places in coral or among pieces of rock are essentialy in the aquarium. As regards the tank floor, very fine sand is not a good choice, as it tends to promote contamination. The coarser grades are much better. As their name suggests, butterfly fishes are rather delicate creatures, and a few years ago it was considered almost impossible to raise them in aquaria. With recent developments in aquarium chemistry and improved aquarium implements, however, it is now relatively easy to keep these fishes alive and well in a tank. A life span of as much as four to six years in an aquarium is no longer considered unusual. Although butterfly fishes are not very resistant to bacteria, conscientious daily aquarium care it usually sufficient to keep them active and healthy. Grindal worms, small pieces of mussel, live brine shrimp, and *Enchytraeus* worms, as well as the better dry foods for marine species, make excellent nourishment for these fishes.

However, three of the most beautiful butterflies that are available are also the most delicate and require quite special case during their first few weeks in the aquarium.

These are *Chaetodon trifasciatus, C. ornatissimus,* and *C. larvatus*. These fish, even though they may feed heavily, they often eventually die. It is obvious that standard aquarium fare provides an insufficient diet for these fish. Living coral and mussels seem to prolong the inevitable, but it is a rarity to hear of these fish living over a year. Butterfly fishes love strong currents, which can be simulated in the tank with the aid of a centrifugal pump. Strong aeration and frequent partial water changes are also important. The more crowded the aquarium, the more frequent the water changes and the more thorough the aeration should be. As regards tank illumination, butterfly fishes are real light-loving fishes. They prefer aquaria which are as bright and sunny as possible. Like most marine species, butterfly fishes are rather sensitive with in regard to water conditions. Although these fishes can survive in water with a specific gravity of as much as 1.025, it is best to keep them in water with a specific gravity of 1.020-1.023. The optimum water temperature for butterfly fishes is around 26-30 °C (79-86 °F) and by no

Heniochus nigrirostris is a rarely seen species of marine butterfly. It is one of the few butterflies found off the west coast of the United States.
Photo: E.Taylor

means should the pH in the tank be allowed to drop below pH 8. Either natural or artificial seawater may be used.

One of the most popular butterfly species is the threadfin butterfly fish *(Chaetodon auriga).* This fish is somewhat less delicate than other butterfly fishes and is found both in the Pacific and the Red Sea. The four-eye butterfly fish (C. *capistratus),* with the large false „eye" near the base of the tail, is a favorite among marine hobbyists in the United States. Other species kept by aquarists include the redstriped butterfly fish (C. *lunula),* the Pakistani butterfly fish (C. *collare),* and the pearlscale butterfly fish (C. *chrysurus*).

In general, butterflies of the genus *Heniochus* adapt *very* readily to aquarium foods and conditions. These highfinned fishes become quite tame and grow rapidly. One letter received from a California hobbyist questioned why his favorite butterfly, *Heniochus nigrirostris,* was not mentioned more often. He felt that such a well-known and hardy species would be an excellent choice for the aquarist who is just beginning to work with butterflies. Although this species is, indeed, hardy, it is well-known mainly to those hobbyists on the west coast of the United States. *Heniochvs nigrirostris is* moderately abundant in the warm waters of the Gulf of California and Baja California but it is collected commercially only to a limited extent. Should *H. nigrirostris* become readily available, it will quickly take its place as one of the more popular marine butterflies.

Based on an article by P.Chlupaty

Breeding coral fishes

When it comes to fish breeding, most marine hobbyists do not set themselves particularly over-ambitious targets. Although freshwater enthusiasts more or less take it for granted that they will manage to breed event the most sensitive tropical fish, marine specialists are happy if they can keep alive for some time a rare species, or one that has always been considered unsuitable for the home aquarium. Unfortunately, many hobbyists succumb to a sort of collecting mania that induces them to buy whatever the importers are offering. This in turn encourages irresponsible importing of rare and delicate species, of which only one individual in ten or twenty will manage to survive on its substitute food. In such cases the question must arise as to whether

Amphiprion frenatus: pair tending brood of eggs. *Photo: K. Paysan*

keeping these species is to be encouraged. Furthermore, attempts at breeding marine fishes fail not least due to the fact that often only individual specimens can be kept-since our aquaria are often much too small for several specimens of the same species.

Very few marine aquarists have dedicated themselves to systematic attempts at fish breeding, and restrict themselves to species with which there are some prospects of success. Accordingly, records of successful breeding of marine fishes are relatively unusual in aquarium literature. To be more precise: after looking through a ten year sequence of aquarium literature between 1970 and 1980 I could come up with only a handful of accounts of really successful breeding of coral fishes. But with the enormous technical improvements of the last few years, a

A colony of yellow cup corals (Tubastrea aurea) *Photo: P. Wilens*

number of the obstacles that previously hampered the successful breeding of coral fishes have now been overcome. We have already had numerous coral fishes spawn in the Stuttgart Aquarium, and fry actually hatched from most of the batches of eggs (although as a rule the young fish were so small that any existing food was too large for them to handle). And even if the young are big enough to cope with freshly hatched *Artemia* nauplii, this doesn't mean that the battle is won. The Japanese pinecone fish *(Monocentrus japonicus)* has spawned in Stuttgart on a number of occasions. The pelagic eggs are easily collected and incubated under artifical conditions. At temperatures of about 25 °C the fry, which are gigantic for a marine fish, hatch after a few hours. However, we have never yet seen the young *Monocentrus japonicus* take food. What could be the reason for this? Have we still not found the right food? Or do the young fish migrate into the ocean depths immediately, despite the fact that numerous marine fish gothrough a planktonic phase? Doubtless it is our lack of knowledge that is to blame for our failures. But perhaps we will get to the root of the problem with this, and other, species one day. Nevertheless, it is quite possible to breed some marine fishes. It was as long ago as 1962 that Casimir and Herkner reported the first success in tank-breeding the peacock blenny *(Blennius pavo)*. More recently Beuret and Studer have again reported successful breeding of numerous *Blennius pavo* at the Basle Zoo. In 1967 Hackinger described the first captive breeding of anemone fish, and in 1969 Stuttgart Aquarium also succeeded in raising large number of *Amphiprion akallopisus* and *A. ephippium.* After a lengthy break we have started to breed anemone fishes again in Stuttgart, and our success has been startling. Our present score stands at several hundred young *Amphiprion frenatum* - and we're still continuing.

In the U.S.A. they also breed an extremely wide range of *Amphiprion* species by the thousands for distribution through the trade, and the first of these are now turning up in Europe.

Furthermore, breeding sea horses and sea urchins does not present too many problems these days, and we have some reason to hope that other species will soon follow. However, as it is the *Amphiprion* species, together with sea horses, that the amateur is more likely to succeed with, these are the subjects that I intend to concentrate on in this article.

Companions for the breeding fishes

Sea horses are placid, peaceful creatures that are best kept as individual pairs in a tank of perhaps ten fishes in all. The other fishes in the tank should also be delicate and gentle sorts that do not present too

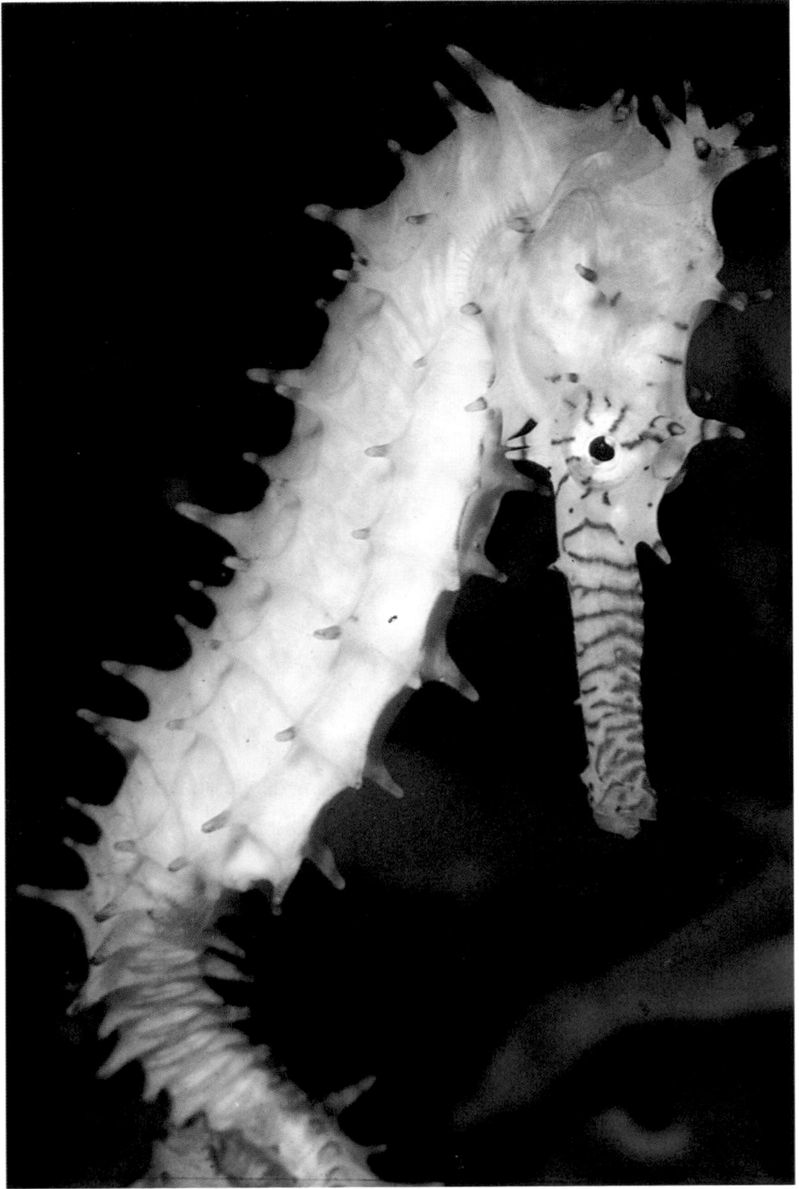

Sea horses breed regularly at the Stuttgart Aqaurium. *Photo: K. Paysan*

much competition over food with the sea horses. On no account should fish with a voracious appetite be put in, as these will dominate the tank at feeding time, with the sea horses not getting a chance. If the sea horses like their surroundings, it will not be long before they reproduce. The young, about a quarter inch long, should be removed and put into a separate rearing tank.
Pairing in anemone fishes is not necessarily such a peaceful affair, but if one buys a group of young fishes of a particular species, a pair is sure to form out of it. At this point it is best to remove the other fishes from the aquarium. The male can be distinguished at a glance from the much larger female. An interesting feature of anemone fishes is that they come into the world as males. It is the dominant specimen of a group that turns into a female, with the others remaining as males. If the female dies, the dominant male takes her place: it turns into a female, and what was previously a subordinate male moves up a step in ranking. However, some years may pass until young pairs start to spawn in the aquarium.
Our anemone fishes (not all of which need anemones in the aquarium) will spawn in 25-50 U.S. gallon tanks, where they seek out a place to spawn and that site they will usually use repeatedly. Before any spate of egglaying, it is carefully cleaned and vigorously defended. In the period from November to May our fish spawn about once a fortnight and guard the developing embryos religously. They rummage around amongst the eggs, removing any that have died and fan fresh water on to the eggs. The young hatch after 8-10 days, about an hour after nightfall. It is at this point that the parental care ceases and the young lose no time in making their way to the surface where they can be lured into shoaling together with the aid of a torch, and then removed into a rearing tank. The parents then clean off the spawning ground and may soon produce a fresh batch of eggs. Initially the young are a bright silver, but quickly turn dark and start to change colour after a fortnight. At about four weeks old the youngsters leave the uppermost surface area in which they lived to begin with and become spread throughout the whole tank.
As long as they have sufficient food they grow at a fast rate and after 4-5 months the largest will be some two inches long, the assumption always being that the food is both suitable and available in adequate quantities.

Food for marine fish fry

Flagellates, ciliates, rotifers and other micro-organisms (often termed 'infusorians') are probably the first food of many marine fishes, although some probably also feed on tiny algae ('green water').
Since providing these foods in sufficient numbers can be difficult, it is

Half inch long young specimens of Amphiprion frenatus, bred in the Stuttgart Aquarium. *Photo: K.Paysan*

the correct feeding of marine fry that is a major hurdle facing hobbyists wishing to rear marine fish.

With much trial and error, it took some time before an 'ideal' food for marine fish fry was discorvered, and the name of this food is *Euplotes.* Like the slipper-animalcule *Paramecium,* it is a ciliate and is more or less similar in size. Breeding quantities of them is an easy matter. Half a teanspoonful of *Tubifex* or dry fish food in 2 1/2 U.S. gallons of salt water produces a splendid culture medium for bacteria, which reproduce rapidly and serves as food for the *Euplotes,* cultures of which are available from biological supply companies.

After as little as two weeks there is sufficient food for the young fishes. Timely transfer of samples of the culture to fresh jars will keep the *Euplotes* culture thriving. Of late, things have been made even simpler, as there is now a tube food available for producing the ciliate culture. Together with *Euplotes,* one should

Euplotes, from above and below, an ideal first food for anemone fish fry.
Photo: REM/Kage

also give special mention to the rotifer, *Brachionus* which is also easy to raise on the abovementioned tube food. Granted, these do not multiply as quickly as *Euplotes*, and if one contaminates the *Brachionus* culture with *Euplotes by* mistake, the *Brachionus* culture will usually die out in time. After about 10 days the food of the fish fry can be switched to newly hatched *Artemia.* Even though sea horses can feed on *Artemia* from a very early age, better survival of sea horses fry seems to follow their initial rearing on foods like *Euplotes or Brachionus.*

After about two to three weeks the fry of *Amphiprion* will feed readily on good quality flaked food (eg. *TetraMarin),* and their growth is usually rapid.

Water quality and tank size

A major problem, especially if one intends to breed coral fishes, is the condition of the water. In undersized marine aquaria (under 25 U.S. gallons), fluctuations in the water quality can be so severe that it is almost impossible to keep sea creatures successfully. But even in large aquaria the water is subject to an ageing process, which it is essential to monitor and control. Whereas stretches of fresh water (as a result of their often small size) are subject to quite drastic seasonal or even daily fluctuations of temperature and water chemistry, the marine environment is extremely stable and (except in estuaries and other brackish areas) fluctuates very little. For this reason the coral fishes (and other inhabitants of the oceans of the world) are not very adaptable- and must be provided with stable, ideal conditions in the aquarium.

Now since every water change in the aquarium can lead to a precipitous alteration to the water quality, the largest possible tank is needed, particularly with delicate, young fishes. Here only a very small proportion of the water needs to be regularly changed. For instance, at Stuttgart we rear our young anemone fishes in large 200 U.S. gallon tanks that are densely colonised with *Euplotes* and *Brachionus,* and contain countless other microorganisms as well. The adults live in pairs in 25 U.S. gallon tanks. After 10 days, once we start feeding *Ar-*

temia, the water is already almost clear, with the greatest proportion of the ciliates and rotifers eaten. To begin with it is not necessary to change the water in these large rearing tanks, and the young fishes will grow almost without casualties. Any small sea horses that need a certain food density and are very difficult to keep a check on in a large tank, should be put into small plastic tanks that are floated in the main tank and into which water is pumped from the large aquarium by an air lift or siphon. Windows of fine perlon gauze should be set into the walls of the smaller tank in order to prevent the food and fishes being swilled away. In this way you have the advantages of the large aquarium and stable water quality, but can still keep a close check on the young fishes. This is not necessary with free swimming *Amphiprion* fry. They are easily seen and their feeding can be concentrated on a confined area with a spotlight.

As you can see, a start has already been made with coral fish breeding and it is hoped that we will now make meaningful progress in this field, to which all serious marine aquarists can contribute. There's a long way to go- but it is not as difficult as it once seemed!

by Dr. Jauch of the Stuttgart-Wilhelma Aquarium

Feeding marine fishes

Fishes need a constant supply of the proper foods to provide energy for immediate use, promote growth, permit the animal to store material for future energy needs, and to resist disease. The proportion of proteins, fats, carbohydrates, minerals and vitamins that each kind of fish requires in its diet is reflected in its feeding habits. What proves an adequate diet for one fish might be completely unacceptable for another. One of the major difficulties encountered in keeping saltwater fishes is in providing a nutritional diet in the right form for each species. Carnivores require a high amount of protein in their diet; this can be supplied by such animal materials as fish, shrimp, scallop, and beef heart. Herbivores require adequate quantities of carbohydrates provided from plant sources. Foods such as algae, chopped spinach, and green peas meet these demands. Omnivores need both plant and animal material in their diet. Some flexibility in the diet of all fishes is important, because each item in it may supply a slightly different composition of proteins, minerals and vitamins, etc., thereby fulfilling the nutrient requirements. The more varied the food which a fish eats, the healthier it should be. Most kinds of fishes which refuse every item of-

The red tail surgeon, Acanthurus achilles, will even eat from the hand when it has been acclimated. Photo: K.Paysan

The lemon or Hawaiian surgeon (Zebrasoma flavescens) in their Hawaiian home. Like other surgeons, they are great algae-eaters and benefit from the use of a vegetable-based flake in the aquarium.

Photo: IKAN/Rödiger

fered except one favorite will suffer from malnutrition. The general categories of foods which are aquarist can offer his marine fishes are live foods, natural foods, and prepared foods.

The *live foods* most commonly available are brine shrimp, *Tubifex* worms, white worms, earthworms, small fishes, and algae. Acceptable live foods which are not as available include *Daphnia,* bloodworms and coral. One or more of these live foods will be eaten by most kinds of marine fishes. All of these foods have good nutritional value, and some provide additional benefits. Brine shrimp will usually live in the marine aquarium until eaten. Live coral and algae are significant elements on a living reef, and are important to certain species of angel and butterfly fishes which eat these foods exclusively. Many of the oth-

A pufferfish love tablet foods like TabMin. This fish is Canthigaster jactator from the Gulf of California. Photo: IKAN/H.Debelius

er live foods will live only briefly in seawater; it is important that they be consumed immediately or removed from the tank to avoid contamination.

Natural foods are here defined as those which have been prepared from the living form without being cooked or dried. They are usually purchased in fresh or frozen condition from a local seafood market, grocery store, or aquarium dealer. Such foods as fish, scallop, crab, shrimp, spinach, green peas, frozen brine shrimp, and beef heart are the most popular. The forms of meat that carnivorous and omnivorous fishes are able to digest most effectively are the flesh of invertebrates and fishes. All fresh foods should be washed clean before feeding, with all fat, bones and fibrous material removed. Frozen foods provide the most nutrition when fed frozen. It

does not discomfort fishes to feed them frozen food in small pieces, so there is no need to thaw the food before feeding. The prepared *foods* normally used for marine fishes are the formulated dry and freeze-dried foods in the form of flakes, powder, pellets, chunks, and whole freeze-dried animals. If a high quality prepared foods is selected, such as *TetraMarin,* it can be an important part of the fish's diet. Not only will it provide the proper proteins and carbohydrates, but it will supply valuable vitamins and trace elements which the fish may not otherwise receive. Prepared foods are easy to feed and normally are available to everyone. Fishes trained to eat commercially produced food will never need to go hungry when live or natural foods are not available. Marine fishes have a high body metabolism, and this requires a constant source of energy. On the reef, fishes spend most of their time foraging for food. Small quantities of food offered at two-hour intervals would be an ideal feeding shedule, but this is impractical for most hobbyists. Feeding two to four times a day is quite adequate, as long as the fishes are allowed to eat their fill. This does not mean that a great amount of food should be placed in the tank all at once. Food that is not eaten will spoil quickly and contaminate the tank. Any excess food

◄ Cleaner wrasse pick parasites from other fish, which is a useful role in the aquarium

should be removed immediately after feeding. It is better to feed small portions at a time and observe the fishes until they have consumed all the food. Then feed again, and continue to do so sparingly until each fish has obviously satisfied his appetitie. Most marine fishes will reach a saturation point at which they refuse to eat any more.
It is common practice to feed fishes by picking up the food by hand and dropping it into the tank. This method is not advisable, particularly when feeding a marine aquarium. Seawater is easily contaminated by foreign substances which may be on a person's hands. The safest method is to handle the food only with a clean utensil, or by wearing sanitary gloves. If the aquarist wishes to feed by hand, he should first wash and rinse his hands. This point may seem ridiculous but it can save the aquarium inhabitants from the addition of toxicants to their environment. It is also important to realize that food placed indiscriminately into the tank may be completely devoured by the dominant members of the community, leaving nothing for the shy members. The food should be placed so that every fish gets his share. A final suggestion indirectly related to feeding techniques is to avoid smoking near a marine tank. Nicotine is poisonous to fishes; only a trace of it in the water can cause disaster.

by P. Green

Experiences with trigger fish

The Balistidae or trigger fish are amongst the most popular subjects in the whole range of marine aquarium fish.

The trigger fish are to the marine fish specialist what the cichlids are to the freshwater enthusiast. Both families are characterised by their intelligence and often unpleasant nature. Of course, there are exceptions that prove the rule.

The trigger fish are so called because the first and second spiny rays of the dorsal fin form a trigger mechanism. The first spine is erectile and can be locked into position by the second and cannot be forced down. So the dorsal fin can be erected whenever danger threatens (eg can be used to wedge the fish in a crevice, thus avoiding capture).

These fish have strong gnawing jaws and teeth and these hard beaks enable them to crack open mussel shells, small crabs, snails, pieces of coral and sea urchins, almost like cracking open nuts. The sea urchins are blown over by a jet of water and are eaten from the unprotected belly side. Molluscs are usually attacked and eaten, so it is inadvisable to keep trigger fish together with lower animals.

In spite of these little vices, many species can be kept successfully as individual specimens in 'fish only'

Red-toothed trigger fish, Odonus niger. *Photo: K.Paysan*

Rhinecanthus aculeatus, the Picasso trigger Photo: K.A.Frickhinger

tanks. They are robust and tenacious creatures. Unfortunately some of them grow very large (up to 24 inches) and are then only suitable for public aquaria.

As their bodies are heavily armoured and not particularly manoeuvrable they cannot be classed amongst the acrobats of the underwater world. Their main means of propulsion lies in the dorsal and anal fins which move like small propellers in a similar fashion to the cowfish or puffer fish. In the aquarium most species readily take to their food, which should be as varied as possible. The diet should contain mussels, freshwater snails, ox-heart, shrimps, *TabiMin* and *Tetratips*. The hard shelled animals will help to keep the teeth worn down. All the aforementioned foods may be enriched with vitamins in liquid form.

My first trigger was an *Odonus niger* which is really placid. It is one of the few which associates naturally in shoals. In the aquarium, it proves to be a lively swimmer, always on the move and always on the look-out for a snack.

On one occasion a "good friend" made me a present of a small *Balistapus undulatus* (orange-green trigger fish). From what he said I gathered that he didn't have room for it in his tank any more.

Being just a novice in the hobby of marine aquaria at the time, I was thrilled with the little fellow. But my joy was shortlived. In a very short time he had grown an inch and began to throw his weight around in a most aggressive manner. In no time at all he had despatched a Pakistan butterflyfish and a long nosed butterflyfish to the great aquarium in the skies, whereupon I decided to hand him on to someone else! Not without first pointing out his little idiosyncrasies though! Since then he has spent the last 6 years in solitary confinement in a 120 U.S. gallon tank. For many years now I have had a lot of pleasure form a very commonly kept trigger fish of the *Rhinecanthus* group. Of course, I am refering to *Rhinecanthus aculeatus,* the Picasso trigger. This is one of the more easily kept species, often being confused with *R .rectangulatus,* the harlequin trigger. The third of the trio, *R. triangulus, is* also an attractive addition to the aquarium. *Balistes caroliniensis is* usually only seen in public aquaria. This fish is just as much at home in the Mediterranean and off the North American coast as in the Caribbean. The following species can also be classed as harmless; *Melichthy ringes,* the blackfinned trigger fish, whose favourite food in the wild consists of sponges, and *Balistes vidua,* the pink-tail trigger.

Balistes caroliniensis, the grey trigger *Photo: P.Stadik*

The queen trigger fish, *Balistes vetula,* which grows to a formidable size, usually proves to be a good-natured occupant of the aquarium. It is inclined to eat a vegetarian diet and likes thawed out salad, although it does not dislike crabs and sea urchins.

What for many people is still a dream fish-*Balistes conspicillum,* the leopard trigger-is not only one of the most expensive, but also one of the most aggressive species. Just as intolerant a companion is the blue-striped trigger, *Pseudobalistes fuscus,* from the Indo-Pacific and the Red Sea, which eats sabellid fan worms in preference. As you can see, there are food specialists amongst the trigger fish, and these are usually the least tolerant species in the aquarium.

In conclusion, I should just like to make an appeal to all marine aquarists. Please try to keep mainly those species which are still relatively common and leave the rarer varieties to public aquaria and zoos. Don't encourage the pillaging of our coral reefs for the sake of personal prestige.

by P. G. Stadik

Balistes vetula, the queen trigger

Beneath the Caribbean

In mid-summer, during July and August, the waters of the Caribbean offer interesting prizes for the aquarist willing to try snorkeling. Later in the year tropical marine fish will be too big for the sparse inshore shelter, but now as young fish, they are near shore and predators such as the foot long *Charanx ruber* move through the shoals scattering fish and hunting food.

The fish in the photographs in this article, were caught by me, quickly put in a small aquarium, photographed and released. In three weeks of combined hunting and photography there were no losses although it was necessary to change one or two buckets full of water in the 16 gallon tank daily. In spite of this drastic water change, the nitrite content rose to more than 0.5 mg per liter and this level was caused by the very fine sand on the aquarium floor. By the end of my holiday the bottom of the tank smelled distinctly of rotting eggs. Let me warn the beginning marine aquarist again: fine sea sand is unsuitable for a marine tank!

There is a tremendous variety of fishes in the area, although not as great as in the Indian or Pacific Oceans, and the multitude of colorful fish you see here will thrill the heart of any aquarist. A few yards from the hotel, on the edge of a

A look at the Caribbean. The shallow waters where the fish are caught.
Photo: H. Baensch

Cardinalfish, *Apogon maculatus* Photo: B. Kahl

spreading band of seaweed you can see many fish. On the way to the weed I swam past the landing dock and below it could see small swarms of five-inch sergeant-major fish *(Abudefduf saxatilis)*. They were hinding beneath the piling and on each upright log there were also coral shrimps *(Stenopus hispidus)*. They raised little claws in defense as I approached. Sergeant-majors are not easy to catch: you need practice and speed or a large net. They occur in all tropical seas in such numbers exporters ship them to European markets.

On the way to the seaweed, swimming slowly above the fine, white sand, I passed rocks which seemed to be hollowed, weathered coral. As I swam closer a few brilliant blue and yellow fish moved from me like bolts of lightening. They were fish called beau gregory, *(Eupomacentrus leucosticus), a* cheek damselfish, about four inches long. They are plentiful in shallow, sandy areas. In holes in the riddled rocks, we found other fish, the grey surgeon fish *(Acanthurus chirurgus),* which found sanctuary not only in deep holes but in empty beer cans scattered along the bottom. They were easy to catch: I simply picked up a can and if there was a surgeon fish inside, put him in the plastic bag at my side. The grayish brown fish are inconspicuous but easy to keep. Their brighter brother, the powder blue tang, *(Acanthurus leucostenon),* which is bright yellow in youth and a magnificent blue as it ages, is much rarer. Both fishes grow to be about one foot long but the young, in August, are rarely more than two inches. They live handsomely on algae and other nutritious vegetable foods.

As I swam further seaward I saw a rectangular block of concrete with two holes on the bottom. One was home to a French angel fish, *(Pomacanthus paru).* He was about two inches long, and rare since I had never seen the species so close to shore. Later I saw them in sheltered places close to the beach and in several areas on the reef. They are beautiful fish, with black and yellow striped bodies, but are not hardy. When caught and shipped they often suffer from hunger.

I was close to the seaweed now. The roots of the plants worked deep into the sand and the leaves were moving back forth with the rhythm of the waves. The bank offered a variety of cover and many fish were there. Beau gregory were plentiful, fiercely defending territory against others of their species, and beyond schools of parrotfish. In some cases

A coral bluehead, Thalassoma bifasciatum *Photo: B.Kahl*

I saw schools of several hundred. The young are inconspicuous and I barely paid attention to them although the adults are almost irridescent.

I sank toward the bottom so that I could see into the caves below the roots, and suddenly was among parrotfishes, red "coral fish", nearly two inches long. Beyond, deeper in the reef adults were four inches long. The fish are rarely imported because they are sensitive to travel and require quantities of oxygen. You catch them with nets, with the opening downward so the fish cannot escape. You rise to the surface slowly, breathe and dive again to bring the fish up gently to help them acclimate. They seem sensitive to changes in pressure. Nearby I found two species of *Apogon* or cardinalfishes and in addition to the common *Apogon maculatus,* the flamefish, there was another without black patches but with a dark brown spot on its caudal peducle.

The highhat *(Equetus acuminatus)* as well as the somewhat rarer *Equetus lanceolatus* can be found only as an adolescent in shallow water in summer and autumn. Even after numerous dives I discovered only one, a fine specimen about ten inches long.

It was in the seaweed that I made my first acquaintance with *Chaetodon* or the butterfly fish. The ones I saw were not as brilliantly colored as species in the Pacific and Indian Oceans, but still unmistakably members of the family. I saw four *Chaetodon capistratus* and nearly as many C. *striatus* in the 100 yards ahead. They are fast, intelligent fish and cannot be captured with a simple net: you need more sophisticated methods. All of the butterfly

A cardinalfish, Apogon erythrinus Photo: H.Baensch

Thalassoma bifasciatum over beautiful coral in the Caribbean Sea.

fish in the Caribbean, including *Chaetodon ocellatus,* are usually found in pairs, often one large fish followed by a smaller oner.

The fish do pair for long periods but the young I saw were barely two or three months old and certainly not sexually mature.

I began to tire of the seaweed. There were sea urchins below, as well as some large five-armed starfish, brown, red and green in color. A few feet beyond, with the hotel still in view, I discovered brown bladder kelp floating on the surface and swam to it. I hoped fish had taken cover in it.

I was surprised. Fifty yards from shore I had found a cornucopia of corals and swarms of fishes, and now, at low tide, it was possible to stand on the sea bed. The water came just above my knees. I had found the remains of a reef that had died.

Coral blueheads *(Thalassoma bifasciatum),* were romping around me in schools and some nipped at the hairs on my legs gently. It was a tingling feeling.

The females and young fish are plain white and yellow with black stripes along their sides, but the full-grown males are magnificently colored. I shooed them away and cut open a sea urchin. Its yellowish eggs are delicacies and the fish were so greedy and preoccupied with the eggs they failed to notice my net dropping over them. I quickly caught many.

Other fish were attracted by the smell of food including surgeon fish and various species of reef fish.

Swiftly I caught one charming fellow, *Eupomacentrus dorsiponiceus,* the orange headed damsel. Only the young are brightly colored and as adults turn a dull grey. In the right terrain you can find one every 100 square feet. The fish does well in an aquarium, living alone in small caves just as it does in the Caribbean. For more than one year I have kept two in an aquarium, feeding them exclusively on *TetraMarin.*

There were other species of reef fish also in the seaweed. *Eupomacentrus flavilatus,* the bicolor damsel. As a young fish it often shows three colors, a yellow belly, grey across the front two-thirds and pink at the rear, but with age the yellow disappears. You care for these as you would other damsels. The fish is very territorial, defending its sites, but unfortunately it is rare.

by Hans Baensch

Setting up a marine invertebrate aquarium

To begin with let us consider the general life support systems that are required to keep most aquatic invertebrates alive in the aquarium. Inevitably some form of water filtration has to be used to help control the levels of dissolved organic pollutants in the water, and/or to ensure good water clarity. Ordinary subsand or undergravel filtration, perhaps assisted by power filtration, is often adequate for single tank displays, although for larger displays, filter systems serving several tanks can be made or purchased from commercial suppliers. Nowa-

Amphiprion ocellaris. *Photo: H.Debelius*

The dottyback is a good fish for the invertebrate aquarium
Photo: H.Debelius/KAN

days neat and efficient filter system 'packages' are also available from specialist dealers, and these can include all the components required to maintain aquatic invertebrates under very stable conditions. Protein skimming is often considered to be an important part of any marine aquarium filtration system and this also includes invertebrate tanks. Nonetheless, no filtration system can really replace the need for regular small scale water changes (see below). Tank turnover times should reflect the needs of the animals in question. In tanks containing tropical reef invertebrates (where environmental stability is important), it is not uncommon to have a turnover time of once every two hours or so, whilst a wide range of temperate marine (and freshwater) invertebrates can be maintained in tanks with a turnover time of (perhaps) several times a day - so long as the water does not become too warm (see below). Good water circulation within the tank, aeration and additional water turbulence can be important from the animal welfare and aesthetic point of view. Imaginative use of air pumps operating airstones can achieve adequate circulation and aeration, and water pumps and/or small dump buckets can greatly improve water turbulence. Excluding the commonly cultured shellfish, relatively few data exist on the tolerance of aquatic invertebrates to pollutants such as ammonia, nitrite and nitrate. It is often assumed that for long term maintenance, levels similar to those recommended for fish are acceptable for most aquatic invertebrates. Nitrates, however, may be one pollutant to which some invertebrates such as corals are relatively sensitive. As a result, levels of nitrate-nitrogen below 20 mg/l are often recommended. Of course, copper and pesticides such as metriphonate (trichlorfon) are among the chemicals commonly used to treat fish diseases, but which are toxic to many invertebrates.

Maintenance of their preferred temperature is a major consideration when keeping aquatic invertebrates. Animals requiring a temperature higher than ambient (ie for most tropical species) can be maintained using standard aquarium heater thermostats, with larger corrosion resistant heating panels available for the heating of large seawater systems. Contact of the animals with the heater may have to be prevented either by situating it in an out of tank reservoir, or by using tank decor, polythene screening, etc.

For some invertebrates (ie some temperate species) the maintenance

Fishes and invertebrates in harmony

Photo: H.Debelius

Actinia equina, a temperate anemone *Photo: H. Debelius*

cooling a relatively small volume of water. New or reconditioned beer chillers can often be obtained at little or no cost from local breweries, and when used in conjunction with a power filter will also chill small volumes of water. Adequate insulation including double glazing will facilitate the maintenance of a desired temperature, and reduce condensation, with chilled tanks.

Lighting techniques are very important from the aesthetic viewpoint, but should, of course, reflect the natural requirements of the animals in question. Some aquatic invertebrates prefer quite subdued lighting, although some coelenterates such as certain tropical corals, anemones, etc., require bright light if they are to thrive. However, a combination of tungsten spot lighting and/or natural spectrum fluorescent tube lighting is often adequate for many of the species preferring quite dim conditions (such as many temperate forms), whilst metal halide lighting (2-5 watts per gallon) is preferred for the illumination of many of the commonly kept coral reef invertebrates. Fluorescent tubes of narrow spectral qualities, for example 'actinic blue' tubes, are considered by some to be beneficial in the keeping of some tropical reef invertebrates, although supporting evidence is largely lacking. When choosing a lighting system for an exhibit of reef invertebrates it is important to bear in mind the nature and intensity of the light experienced by these animals in the wild, and attempt to duplicate this in the aquarium. Some deeper water coral reef invertebrates may prefer relatively dim conditions.

Tapwater can be an adequate water supply for most invertebrates, so long as temperature shock and excessive levels of, for example chlorine and pesticides, can be avoided. (Some freshwater invertebrates such as crayfish do prefer quite hard water though). Natural seawater, or synthetic seawater made from a good quality dry mix plus tapwater, are both satisfactory for most marine invertebrates. However, some temperate shellfish seem to be tolerant of quite basic artificial salt water recipies, whilst it is generaly assumed that many coral reef invertebrates require a complex artificial mix that attempts to duplicate natural seawater. The addition trace element supplements and/or regular partial water changes with fresh seawater are often recommended for the successful maintenance of many marine invertebrates. Regular partial water changes (perhaps 10-30% of the tank volume per month), have the added benefit that they can also help to keep nitrate levels down to an acceptable level. As an example for tropical marine invertebrates, the following display is maintained in a large public aquarium near my home. The 300 gallon tank (24 ins deep) is the main display on a system with a total volume of 1000 gallons and is filtered by two cartridge filters and a high pressure sand filter, with supplemental protein skimming. Water temperature is maintained at around 25 °C with a stainless steel submersible heater. The display tank turnover time is approximately once every two hours, with in-tank aeration and turbulence provided by airstones and a small water pump. The tank contains a range of coral reef invertebrates such as some corals (such as *Goniopora, Plerogyra, Dendronephyta, Xenia, Sarcophyton),* anemones (including *Radianthus, Aiptasia),* carpet anemones (eg *Actinodiscus),* clams *(Tridacna, Lima),* brittle stars and starfish (including *Protoreaster),* sea cucumbers and sea apples (such as *Paracucuamaria),* sea urchins (including *Diadema),* fan worms and tube worms (such as *Sabellastarte),* and shrimps (including *Stenopus hispidus).* Amongst the fish that are kept are damsel fish and clown fish (Pomacentridae), gobies (Gobiidae), blennies (Blennidae, Eleotridae), wreck fish *(Anthias)* and mandarin fish *(Synchiropus).*

Five hundred watts of metal halide lighting is provided for between eight and eleven hours per day, along with two 120 watt 'actinic blue 03' tubes. Tank decor consists of primarily tufa rock along with a luxuriant growth of *Caulerpa* macro-algae. The foods that are offered two to three times a day include frozen brineshrimp and frozen plankton, live brineshrimp (adults and nauplii), live rotifers, fish flaked food, and a suspension of dried invertebrate diet with added trace elements. Whilst variety is important, overfeeding, it seems, can

Invertebrates with small fish Photo: H. Debelius/KAN

precipitate a number of problems, perhaps including the proliferation of *Aiptasia* anemones and various flatworms.

Natural seawater is used in this system and typical water quality characteristics are: pH 8.0, carbonate hardness 7 °dH, total ammonia not detectable, nitrite-nitrogen less than 0.1 mg/l, nitrate-nitrogen 10 mg/l, and specific gravity 1.020. Water changes to the coral reef system as a whole are of the order of 10% per month with regular attention to filter maintenance. Although only used at a low level there is some circumstantial evidence to suggest that the use of ozone in this system may have a detrimental effect on large anemones such as *Radianthus.*

Invertebrates, including those from marine environments, are an incredibly diverse group of animals. In order to achieve greater success in their maintenance under captive conditions, we may have to spend more time and effort considering (and duplicating) their specific environmental requirements.

by C. Andrews

Keeping marine invertebrates

The sea can offer much more to the marine aquarist than just beautiful coral reef fishes. Without the thousands of different invertebrates which live on and are part of the reef, the fishes could not exist. Invertebrates make up about 98 % of all known animals. They are characterized by the lack of any internal skeletal system which would give support to the body. In general, they are small, soft-bodied creatures which must lead a rather sedentary life. A few are covered by a though external shell or exoskeleton. There are more than 25 major groups of invertebrates (phyla), but only a very small percentage of these animals are suitable for the marine aquarium. The most commonly maintained marine invertebrates include the following: (1) Phylum

A beautiful set-up invertebrate aquarium. This will require plenty of illumination and ideal water conditions

Coelenterata or Cnidaria,- sea anemones, corals, and hydroids, (2) Phylum Annelida-tubeworms, (3) Phylum Arthropoda - crabs and shrimps, (4) Phylum Mollusca-snails, bivalves, and nudibranchs, and (5) Phylum Echinodermata-starfish and sea urchins. Since many marine fish feed on invertebrates, it is advisable to be careful when attempting to keep the two types of animals together.

Damselfish and Sea Anemone Aquarium

The well-known symbiotic relationship between sea anemones and certain damselfish or the genus *Amphiprion* is one which merits an environment all its own. Most species of coral reef fishes can be harmed if they come in contact with the tentacles of a sea anemone. These arms contain stinging cells (nematocysts) which are used to paralye prey or defend against predators. Clownfish, however, are able to live in a mutually beneficial relationship with them. On the reef, clownfish are never known to stray far from their particular anemone. The most natural condition, therefore, is to maintain these fish with their invertebrate companions.

Sea anemones are all carnivorous animals, but they are classified according to the size of food they collect. Predatory specimens such as *Stoichactis, Discosoma, Radianthus,* and *Anemonia* feed on fishes and various invertebrates. They will eat

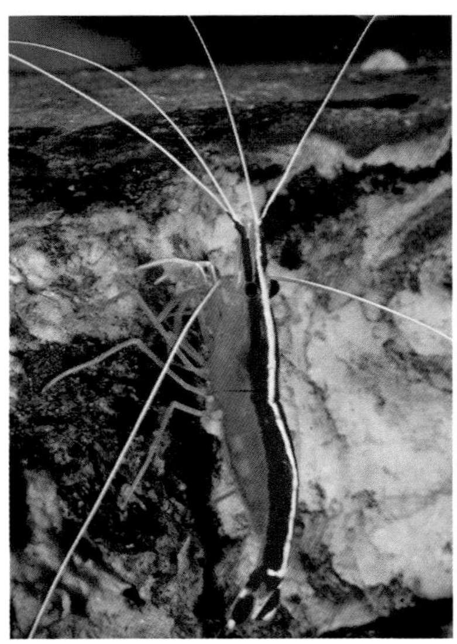

The common, hardy coral shrimp, Stenopus hispidus. Photo: K.Paysan

chunks of fresh or frozen sea foods such as scallop, shrimp, crab, or fish. Also, beef heart, brine shrimp, and pelletized foods will be accepted. Some anemones are known as particle feeders. They will eat only very small living organisms such as brine shrimp nauplii, marine protozoans, *Tubifex* worms, and *Daphnia* . The freshwater foods must be eaten quickly before they die. Particulate feeding anemones are best maintained in strictly invertebrate tanks.

Most symbiotic anemones grow quite large, but only small ones of 10 inches diameter or less should be kept in the aquarium. It is always best to keep anemones by themselves or with their natural companions.

Invertebrate and Non-Predatory Fish Aquarium

If the fish in a community tank containing invertebrates become sick, it may be impossible to add drugs or medicines to the water. Invertebrates are highly susceptible to changes in water chemistry, and treatment of the fish will result in death for the lower animals. Some disease treatments are toxic to marine invertebrates, so only 'safe' treatments must be used. The best fish for the invertebrate aquarium are those which will not harm their tank mates. These include sea horses, pipefish, and certain species of gobies and blennies.

Filter-feeding Invertebrate Aquarium

Many invertebrates must filter their food from the water. Examples are all types of corals, hydroids, barnacles, tubeworms, and most bivalves. Feeding these animals may require the preparation of a mixture of artificial plankton. This is composed of various liquified materials which are of nutritional value to the animals. An organic "soup" of this type can easily pollute the aquarium if too much is added. It is essential that a powerful and effective filter be used to reduce the amount of suspended matter in the water after each feeding. Filter feeders need only be fed liquified foods once every other day. Daily feedings of brine shrimp nauplii are recommended.

Non-Filter Feeding Invertebrate Aquarium

These are probably the easiest invertebrates to maintain in the aquarium. Feeding them is usually little problem, partially due to the fact that most of these animals are highly mobile. Crabs, hermit crabs, shrimps, lobsters, and starfish are carnivores. Most of them will eat pieces of fish, shrimp, crab, beef heart, scallop, and earthworms. Unfortunately, these animals tend to be quite aggressive, and they may fight with or eat their tankmates. Sea anemones and coral polyps are particularly vulnerable to predation. The nudibranchs, or sea slugs, are very unusual creatures which feed on a variety of materials. Some of these are difficult to keep since they refuse to eat anything but their natural specific foods. Sea urchins and many snail-like molluscs are her-

A sea slug is an exotic addition to the invertebrate aquarium.

bivores. The best food for these animals is algae. Actually, the invertebrate tank depends on algae growth not only as a food source, but also as a means of purifying the water.

Mixed Filter and Non-filter-feeding Invertebrate Aquarium

This tank is extremely interesting as it contains many different types of invertebrates. Certain problems might occur due to this variety, but the aquarist will undoubtedly learn from these experiences. A good deal of loss due to predation can be expected. Care must be taken not to pollute the tank when feeding the filter feeders.

Here are a few additional points you should remember:

• Invertebrates are extremely sensitive to changes in water chemistry. They must be acclimated very carefully to a new environment.

• The pH level is very critical; it should be a pH of 7.8-8.2. pH values should not fall below 7.8

• Most invertebrates offered for sale are from tropical waters, and it is preferable that their temperature range be 22-25 °C (72-76 °F).

• Invertebrates can be overcrowded just as easily as fish. A large tank is preferable to a small one, even though some animals are quite small.

• The sessile nature of many invertebrates demands that water circulation be at a maximum level.
Also, water flow should not be restricted to one direction. Water circulation pumps can provide the necessary current. Water should be removed from near the bottom of the tank and returned above the water's surface in a mult-directional flow.

• A large amount of dissolved oxygen is essential. This can be provided by strong water movement, such as by air diffusers or water pumps.

• The filter bed material in an invertebrate tank should be fairly fine, but coarse enough to permit adequate water movement to function as a biological filter. Many animals must dig in the substratum to feed or construct a site to which they can attach themselves.
If the bottom gravel is too coarse, this will be impossible.

• Algae play an important role in the invertebrate aquarium. Proper culturing of this plant life depends on an adequate supply of light. Invertebrates are accustomed to a daily cycle of light and darkness. Many filter feeders will eat only after the lights are turned off. 14-16 hours of light should be supplied each day to encourage algae growth and create diurnal cycle.

by D. Parsons

Disc or carpet anemones in the tropical marine aquarium

Within the Phylum Coelenterata (which includes the jellyfish, corals and anemones) is the sub-class Hexacorallia, itself containing the following orders: stony corals (Scleractinia), cylindrical sea anemones (Ceriantharia), antipatharians (Antipatharia), colonial anemones (Zoantharia) and the sea anemones (Actinaria). The order containing the coral anemones or false - corals (Corallimorpharia) represents an intermediary between the sea anemones and the stony corals. This latter order comprises ten genera, of which the best known representatives are probably the various *Actinodiscus* species.

In this article I should like to discuss four species from three different genera within the coral anemone group which are all well suited for keeping in the marine aquarium. The first two, both shown in the photograph, belong to the A*ctinodiscus* genus. There are about 20 different species in this genus, coming from the tropical areas of the Indo-Pacific and the Red Sea. As the appearance of so many of these representatives is highly similar, it is almost impossible to identify them without a detailed examination.
The first one I would like to mention here, was one of the first I ever

Actinodiscus.

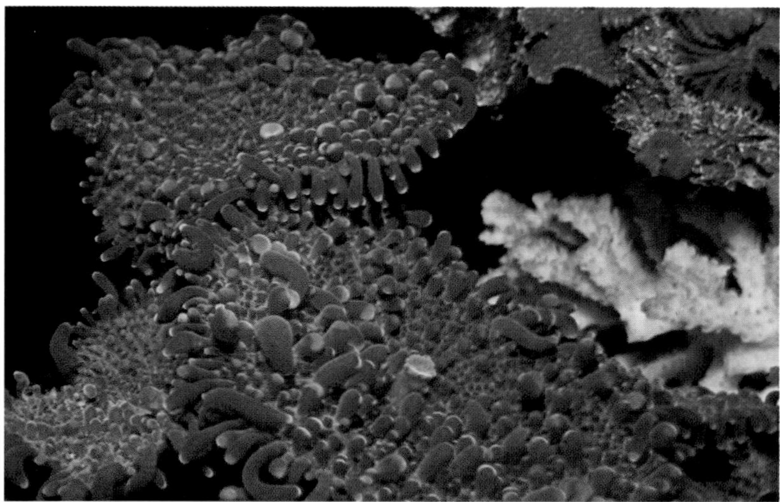

Ricordia is a Caribbean carpet anemone.

kept in an invertebrate aquarium. It's basic colour is light brown with green, iridescent 1/20th inch long tentacles located around the edge of the disc. On the disc itself there are no tentacles but simply ray-like elevations around the slightly raised mouth opening. In normal specimens the diameter often reaches 1-2 ins although certain individuals may grow to 3 ins across. At this size they will divide. This species is obtainable through the trade as a colony of 10 to 40 animals living on limestone. I have never yet come across them as single specimens (see photograph above). They are very easy to keep. Their main requirement is plenty of light, as this promotes the rapid reproduction of their symbiotic algae, the zooxanthellae, living within their tissues. As their staple food I give finely chopped *TetraTips,* along with freezedried prawns, shrimps and mosquito larvae, which are also finely mashed with a mortar and pestle. I also add a vitamin preparation to the mixture. The prepared food is then made into a paste with a little seawater and distributed amongst the individual animals with the aid of a pipette.

The shape of the *Actinodiscus* undergoes some enormous changes during the feeding process. The animals roll themselves up towards their centre until the whole surface is lying over the central column. They then remain fixed in this position until the food in the gastric cavity has disappeared, whereupon they open fully once more.

This species will reproduce often even without supplementary feeding - so long as there is plenty of light. When its diameter reaches 2-3 ins, the disc anemone divides right across its middle, even the mouth splitting in two. In my aquarium this process takes about two weeks and, once completed, the two new individuals migrate a short distance away from each other. I have also been able to observe another form of reproduction. In this method, part of the pedal disc (the base) splits off and a new anemone develops from this. I have not yet had an opportunity of observing any sexual reproductive behaviour. With this rate of reproduction the colony expands continuously and soon extends on to the decorations, thus incorporating any nearby stones into the general ensemble.

The second *Actinodiscus* species (see below) no longer has any form of tentacles. Its basic colour is also brown with a radial pattern of dark green stripes. Both colours result from the zooxanthellae. The mouth opening is even smaller than in the above species and as I have not yet been able to observe any evidence of feeding, I must conclude that this species is very dependent upon good lighting. I came across this species under rather unusual circumstances. There had been a colony of them in our society aquarium for some time, and it was flourishing thanks to the first class lighting system there. As a result, the stone soon became overgrown and certain specimens started to detach themselves and were carried away by the current (anemone tanks should always have some current created by aeration and the filter action). I thought that it must surely be possible to transfer some of these individuals to another aquarium and so I tried it. I selected five of these Ac*tinodiscus* of various sizes and transferred them carefully to my invertebrate aquarium. Here I put them together so that they were in a group and as such were at least approaching their natural conditions. In spite of the strong algal growth, they soon gained a foothold on the coral. In general, the care of this particular variety is very similar to that of the previous one, although its dependence on good lighting is more pronounced. They should, therefore, be kept in the most favourable light conditions as possible. They do not like too powerful a current though. Apart from this they are fairly undemanding.

The third species I should like to mention originates from the Caribbean and is called *Ricordia florida.* These disc anemones are also extremely colonial. It's basic colouring is dark green to brown. It has short tentacles which are so closely packed onto the body that it resembles the gnarled bark of a tree. The outermost tentacles are capable of being extended to quite some length. I obtained my first colony six years ago. At the time it was wedged in between two stems of coral and in my view was quite firmly anchored there. As I had set it directly beneath a light (only 6 ins below the water surface), I was soon able to ob-

serve how new specimens began to break off from the pedal disc, some of which grew over on to the two stems of coral.
At the time I placed several sea urchins into the aquarium to combat the algae. Then, when I got up one morning, I found that the sea urchins had transformed the aquarium to suit their own tastes. Included in their scheme was the disruption of my *Ricordia* colony. One of the disc anemones had been torn away from the mother colony and left hanging on a *Fungia* (mushroom) coral. Clearly, it was time to redesign my marine aquarium to make it as sea urchin-proof as possible and to anchor the anemones more firmly in position. I was a little fearful for one particular disc anemone as it's base, the pedal disc, had been badly torn. For a whole week nothing happened. The disc anemone clung limply on to the stone but then it started to open up fully again and because of its superb size it was soon one of the finest items in my aquarium. Soon, small pieces began detaching themselves from the pedal disc and a year later the infant was larger and more beautiful than it's parent.
These observations led me to commence an experiment four years later. When an elephant's ear *(Rhodactis)* became so overgrown that it was stifling part of the *Ricordia* colony, I carefully detached a specimen and 'transplanted' it alongside a *Tridacna* mussel. I was now able to observe a similar train of events as those that occurred with the detachment form of reproduction, except that the attachment procedure of the new anemone took somewhat longer, namely two weeks. After this, it opened fully once more.
The *Ricordia* disc anemone is in my opinion the most light dependent of all since it will only open in very intense light. This variety also does

Anemones are quiet hardy marine invertebrates.

not appreciate an excessively strong current. I did not see it taking in any additional food in the form of planktonic matter.
The last variety I would like to describe is not a species which forms dense colonies but instead lives in small groups of a maximum of three to four individuals. The animal in question is another representative of the *Rhodactis* genus. These disc anemones - which used to be sold under the name of *Discosoma* - can reach a diameter of 9 ins and more, hence they are sometimes called giant sea anemones. Their basic colouring is dark green to brown.

They have only very short tentacles, not even 1/2 inch long, and it is quite noticeable that these representatives have a narrow, tentacle-free peripheral zone.
It will be readily appreciated that, because of their size, these animals require a lot of space and this should be borne in mind if intending to make a purchase. There is no point at all in placing these creatures just anywhere in the tank decoration because they will soon overlap the other lower animals' which will perish as a result. This species needs a lot of light if it is to attain it's full size. It does not like a strong current. As far as I could tell, it does not accept even finely pulverised food. It is true that particles of food do become lodged between the tentacles but this is eventually rejected if it is not eaten beforehand by my *Zebrasoma* surgeon fish. To begin with the disc anemone was so distressed by the food offered, that it contracted itself up every time it was fed. Since then, however, it has become more accustomed to the food and even allows the surgeon fish to scavenge for it. All the species mentioned here are sturdy creatures which can be considered amongst the hardiest of all the lower animals. Of course, it is essential to try to provide optimum conditions for them, based on good illumination and not too strong a current. I keep my disc anemones in water having a pH around 8.3, density 1.020 and a temperature of 79 °F. Even if kept together with other invertebrates there is a little to worry about, though a certain safety margin of some 4 ins should perhaps be allowed around them. Then they can even be kept in a community tank with such prickly customers as ceriantherians (tube anemones) or *Actinodendrum plumosum.* Disc anemones scarcely disturb other invertebrates at all, so long as they do not spread or overlap into the others' territory which could have fatal results.

Text and photographs by D. Brockmann

Tube anemones

It is not unusual to successfully maintain tube anemones in a marine aquarium for 10 or even 15 years. Three aspects of their care are particularly important:

1. Water
2. Oxygen
3. Food

There are available several excellent synthetic mixtures that produce good quality seawater for the marine aquarium. Regular checks of pH, nitrate and nitrite, along with frequent, partial water changes, all aid in maintaining good water quality for marine fish and invertebrates alike. Marine animals require plenty of oxygen, though the needs of marine invertebrates are often under estimated. In most aerated aquaria the oxygen saturation value amounts to about 60-70% of saturation at most. (At 80 °F, seawater which is 100% saturated at normal air pressure holds between 6-7 parts per million of oxygen).

I no longer use just airstones to provide aeration in my marine tanks.

Tube anemones (Cerianthus) are incredibly beautiful .

Instead I let the filter outflow pass a current of water across the surface: this seems to permit a greater absorption of oxygen from the air, at the same time as not providing a too violent current to disturb the anemones on the tank floor. This method does not, however, appear to increase oxygen saturation above about 70%. It is possible to achieve 100% saturation using hydrogen peroxide. For marine fish I use a 15% solution of hydrogen peroxide, and add one or two millilitres to each 25 gallons of aquarium water. Care must be exercised so that the concentrated peroxide solution does not come into contact with the fish, as it may cause damage to delicate tissues. Invertebrates are even more sensitive to peroxide. When adding it to a marine invertebrate tank, the few millilitres of 15% hydrogen peroxide should be diluted in a half bucket of seawater, and then slowly distributed throughout the aquarium. In order to achieve a constant high level of oxygen saturation, it is necessary to add the above mentioned amounts of hydrogen peroxide to the tank either every day, or every other day. You should soon notice an improvement in the appearance and vitality of your aquarium inmates.

It is often said that the colours of tropical tube anemones fade after some time in an aquarium. I believe that this loss of colour may be prevented by correct feeding . Initially I only fed my anemones on mussel meat, shrimps, fish, etc., but soon realised that this did not seem to be adequate. Therefore, I prepared a sticky paste of *TetraMarin* and seawater, and injected this into the mussel meat, or squeezed it into an empty shrimp case using a disposable syringe (without a needle). This ensured that the anemones consumed all the valuable nutrients contained within *TetraMarin,* and seemed to markedly improve their growth and colour. Some anemones I have had for 18 months and fed in this manner, have shown no loss in colour and (if anything) their overall mystic beauty has improved with time.

Moving on to some other aspects of the care of tube anemones, it is advisable to support these invertebrates in their tank with plexiglass tubes. In this manner they may be fixed in one spot, and new anemones that are obtained without a mantle may be better protected. The plexiglass tube should be glued at an angle to a stone or plate. At the lower end of the tube there must be a hole the same size as the diameter of the tube. The tube should (of course) be somewhat larger than the mantle of the anemone to comfortably accommodate the fast growth of these animals. The tube may be decorated by mixing coloured sand with an artificial resin and hardener. If the plexiglass tube is painted with this mixture you can decorate the tube to suit your own tastes: piecesof coral, mussel shell, snail shells, etc. The aquarium coral sand

Magnificent Cerianthus.

is then heaped up around the open end of the tube, and the anemones will quickly dig themselves into it, rear end first. By using these tubes you can save yourself about 2 inches of depth of sand, though you must remember that the growth of anemones can be quite tremendous. One of my anemones had a mantle some 6 inches in length, which grew to 31 inches in eight months. The growth then tailed off, though as time passed it continued to become much thicker. Tube anemones can be kept in a range of decorative substrates, though they must have the end of their mantle sticking into sand.

These invertebrates can squeeze themselves into the tiniest crevices between rocks, etc., from which they can only be extricated by force. Tropical tube anemones, once injured, are virtually certain to die. More temperate species may often survive this trauma, though the tropical species seem unable to deal with secondary bacterial infection at increased temperatures. Tube anemones can be kept very close together (so that their tentacles touch), provided that they are all off the same species. A commonly available anemone is *Cerianthus membranaceus,* that will mix well with others of the same species. My attempts at keeping C. *membranacus* with other tube anemones from the Philippines have failed. Nonetheless whichever species you keep, you are sure to find the tube anemones fascinating and beautiful inmates for the tropical marine aquarium.

Text and photographs by H. Ruffus

The Swimming Crab, Callinectes sapidus

A biologist friend of mine returned from a study tour in the USA with a number of specimens for me, one of which was a 'blue crab the Latin name of which is *Callinectes sapidus*. The swimming crabs from the family Portunidae, to which the blue crab belongs, can be recognised by the paddle-like broadening of the terminal section of their last pair of legs and, as I was soon to notice, by some other quite destinctive characteristics.

In the USA people are very fond of eating these creatures - and in large quantities at that! An especially popular item - and appropriately priced - is the so called 'soft crab' the stage shortly after sloughing, when the armoured shell is still soft. To satisfy this demand these creatures are kept in pens until they shed their shells and despatched throughout the USA when the time is right.

My blue crab was put into a 20 gallon aquarium together with two *Limulus* or horse shoe crabs. By the next day, and to my great consternation, the *Limulus* were nowhere to be found. Evidently, the blue crab was setting about demonstrating one of the hints featured in an aquarium

The Florida blue crab, Callinectes sapidus, in a typical aggressive pose.

book that I consulted - rather belatedly - that it should be kept singly! However, the crab had set about solving this problem in its own way! Now I give it a daily feed of *Tetra-Tips,* small pieces of fish and deep frozen shrimps to satisfy it's hearty appetite. It was presumably because of a lack of food deliveries that the animal took to setting off on it's own foraging expeditions, that were to take it through the length and breadth of our bedroom. On one of these nocturnal forays it managed to fall behind the cupboard supporting the aquarium, in a spot where it could not, as usual, be rescued by us. After some deliberation we decided to clear out the aquarium, and moved it to one side so that we could pull the cupboard forward and rescue the crab from it's difficult situation. By the time we got things back together again, several hours had elapsed and it was 2 o'clock in the morning before the crab was back in it's aquarium.
From then on we kept the aquarium well covered and the nocturnal wanderings of this fellow - by now 4 ins across - ceased. One night - my wife was on her own as I was in hospital with appendicitis - the blue crab broke the thermometer, causing the contents to be discharged into the tank and contaminate the whole body of water. My wife had to promptly clear out the entire tank on her own, in order to save the blue crab. He had to be given temporary accommodation in a plastic bucket. When I eventually received the ultimatum - „Either the crab goes or I do" - I decided to opt for my wife and handed the animal back to the unsuspecting original donor.
It is still alive today, almost twice the size, in a well covered aquarium in the Biological Department of the University of Stuttgart, without any heating, any thermometer or any other tank inmates to intrude on it's solitude. I had taken the precaution of relating my experience to the new owners. Crabs are fascinating, but can be destructive.

Text and photograph
by W. Baumeister

Our family favourite: Odontodactylus scyllaris, the mantis shrimp

The animal in question is a 6 ins long mantis shrimp of the species *Odontodactylus scyllaris.* This group of animals, very poorly known scientifically, is often available from dealers. For their size, these are among the most ferocious invertebrate predators. The spirited, almost circumspect behaviour and the magnificent colouring of my mantis shrimp, have made it an instant and irresistible attraction for all

The mantis shrimp, Odontodactylus scyllaris *Photo: h: Debelius/KAN*

our visitors. This is all the more so as I have housed it in a 20 gallon tank in a prominent position in my room. I often find that a visitor will try to provoke the shrimp by waggling a finger before the front pane, but once the shrimp emerges from it's den to investigate what's happening, the hand is very quickly withdrawn! This shrimp has remarkably good eyesight. When searching for food it does not use it's relatively short feelers, but it's very mobile eyes. The eyes are large and on stalks as in most other higher crustaceans, and the shrimp is able to move each eye separately, giving it a total and unobstructed view of it's surroundings. It uses it's feelers only to confirm that the morsel is indeed suitable for eating before seizing it with it's pincer-like claws. These mouthparts are made up of two parts; a long shaft with a groove in it's face and an articulating shaft with sharp edges or spines.

The way it catches it's prey is an extraordinary affair. As it's name implies, it is indeed of a similar design to that of the preying mantis.

The mantis shrimp can deal a really painful blow with it's pincers. Despite the fact that it is quite capable of distinguishing between a finger and a food item, I nevertheless exercise a good measure of caution whenever I feed mine by hand as it always swims up to the surface very quickly whenever I put in the food. However, it has never snapped at me yet.

The species *Odontodactylus scyllaris* could never be described as a relentless hunter; it's style consists more of lurking in it's den until it's victim strays close by. This technique is very much in evidence with my specimen. Once it's prey is within close reach it will shoot out and try to push it's body on top of the victim, holding on tight with it's pairs of legs which are positioned behind the pincer-like claws. These three pairs of legs are armed with large claws for this purpose. If this method fails, or if the prey seems to be too large right from the very outset, then it will strike again. My specimen regards any creature up to 4 ins as fair game even snails and large hermit crabs cannot be considered safe! It does not immediately recognise dead food, such as a motionless sand shrimp, as an edible item.

In spite of it's predatory lifestyle and its far from harmless appearance I wouldn't like to be without my mantis shrimp now. As soon as I approach the aquarium it comes up to the front pane and waits for me to feed it. In some instances I might just be doing something in the vicinity of the aquarium and if it doesn't get anything it becomes aggressive and clouts the pane with it's claws. It makes such a noise that it always gives you quite a start. However, because of their predatory nature, they must not be kept together with fish or other invertebrates. They do not bother with anemones or other sessile animals though. Nor does it go for the *Caulerpa* in the tank, although when moulting it cuts great amounts of it to camouflage the entrance to it's cave. It is strange that such a powerful and well armed creature can be practically defenceless for almost 24 hours during moulting.

by Joachim Grosskopf

Keeping anemone shrimps in the marine aquarium

During the last couple of years anemone shrimps and crabs have become increasingly available to the marine aquarist, and I first came across them in the Artis-Aquarium in Amsterdam. I was fascinated by these strange, fragile looking creatures, and for a long time nursed an ambition to keep them, together with their associated anemones, in my own aquarium. Fortunately my dream became reality when I set up a tank designed especially for these tiny marine invertebrates, and I acquired my first *Periclimenes brevicarpalis.*

Periclimenes species occur in almost all temperate and tropical seas throughout the world. *P. brevicarpalis* is from the Caribbean and attains an average length of 1-2 ins excluding the antennae. It is as transparent as glass, with brown, orange and yellow patches on it's back and towards the rear of it's body. According to some these species, like their larger relative *Stenopus hispidus,* should only *be* kept in pairs, but *P. brevicarpalis* certainly behaves peacefully towards other inhabitants of the aquarium. Keeping these shrimps did not prove

The anemone shrimp, Periclimenes brevicarpalis
Photo: D. Brockmann

particularly difficult, and I maintained my 100 gallon aquarium at 78 °F with a pH of 8.3 and a specific gravity of 1.020. Apart from being sensitive to any reduction in oxygen, they are otherwise quite hardy animals. Certainly *P. brevicarpalis* is considerably easier to keep than other shrimps such as *Hippolysmata grabhami,* although they have, of course, to be kept with suitable species of anemones.

As regards feeding these creatures, I soon discovered that flaked food was just as readily accepted as finely chopped mussel, *Tubifex,* etc., although I did have one small problem to overcome. I had been giving my anemones a small lump of mussel at regular intervals, when one day I discovered that the shrimp was catching it himself and leaving the anemone empty handed'! From then on I always put in several pieces at once so that even after he had taken two or three pieces there was still enough for the anemone to claim it's share!

In the wild these shrimps live as commensals with sponges, corals, anemones and other organisms inhabiting coastal waters, although as with many other situations of this kind it is difficult to decide whether the relationship is truely one of symbiosis or commensalism. However, what struck me in particular was that they seem to prefer living with anemones which have powerful stings, an observation also made on a similar situation by several marine invertebrate enthusiasts. When I added a *Crytodendrum* specimen to a *Radianthus,* one of my animals immediately reverted to it's former home when given the opportunity to do so. In my opinion either the shrimp realised that the very strong sting of the *Crytodendrum* provided it with greater protection (and 'realisation' will be the result of natural selection favouring certain behaviour), or it found it easier to live amongst the shorter tentacles of this species; the longer tentacles of the *Radianthus* always seemed about to smother it!

The previous incident also led me to notice another interesting behavioural trait of these shrimps which might interest readers. A pair of *Hippolysmata grabhami* selected as a home the same *Radiantus* specimen which had previously been colonised by my *Periclimenes.* (This in itself was interesting as until then my colleagues and I were not aware that this species also lives as a commensal in these anemones). From the very beginning they were given very little opportunity to assert themselves against their much smaller and outnumbered adversary, and were frequently chased away minus parts of their legs and antennae! However, they were never actually ousted from their intended home and eventually managed to settle down and establish themselves when the *Periclimenes* moved back to the larger *Crytodendrum.* This incident serves to illustrate just how assertive such a small creature can be when defending it's home territory, and remarkably enough it survived injury throughout the numerous confrontations!

When actually frightened, *Periclimenes* shows an interesting defensive behaviour which can often be seen in the aquarium if the little crustacean is disturbed. When startled, for example by a fish, it immediately stretches it's chelicerae forward, lays it's long whip like antennae over it's back, an assumes a position so that it is parallel with the tentacles of the anemone and is holding on only with its third pair of walking legs. This defensive stance is quite effective as the shrimp is now guarded on all sides by it's host, and can ward off any attack from above with it's chelicerae.

The anemone shrimps do not seem to be as closely dependent upon their obliging anemones as are the anemone crabs such as *Neopetrolisthes oshimai,* which only leave their homes when actually forced to do so. In contrast, *Periclimenes* often venture out into their surrounding area, although they rapidly retreat back to the security of their home if danger threatens. At night they often also go off in search of food, and will explore some distance away from their 'base'

by D. Brockmann

Marine invertebrates at home

As the diver descends from the brilliant light of the tropical sun into the bluegreen depths, the beam of his light penetrates the caves and crevices of the reef to reveal a world of strange marine creatures, animals which, although normally hidden from human sight, offer a wonderful display of exotic colours. This living community of sponges, ascidians, and soft, horn moss and stone corals is virtually unique in its diversity of shape and form, and provides an irresistible challenge to the tropical invertebrate enthusiast who wishes to re-create this mysterious world in his marine tank.
After I had been diving several times in the Red Sea and the Indian and Pacific Oceans, I decided to set up an aquarium solely for the invertebrates which I had found in the deeper zones of the coral reefs. These delicate creatures provide a considerable contrast to the shallow water leather corals of the Indo-Pacific reefs, which I described in a previous issues of the *Aquarium Digest.* Using various pieces of rock and some decorative pieces of dead coral, I constructed an underwater landscape which roughly resembled my recollections of the reef. I joined the separate pieces together using a mixture of one part pure Portland cement and three parts of coarse sand, to thus produce stable and easily handled pieces of decor. These were kept in water for three weeks and were then washed with dilute hydrochloric acid (10 parts water to one part acid), after which I placed them in my 44 US gallon aquarium to form an imitation reef, complete with crevices and caves. Finally, I added a 11/2 inch layer of coarse coral gravel after which my underwater landscape looked rather realistic!
Having created a suitable layout in the tank I then installed an efficient protein skimmer and two strong rotary pumps. These pumps had an output of about 250 U.S. gallons per hour which I set up so that they produced the desired water current in the tank. To re-create the peculiar blue-green light which permeates the reef at depths of 35-50 feet I fitted one *Philips* TL 17 green light in the hood. Later on I also added a single 20 watt *Osram* L *36 Natura* light, so that I could enjoy the full brilliance of the animals' colours for the relatively short periods of time that I wanted to take a close look at my collection.
During the next few months the aquarium was allowed to develop a biologically active bacterial flora, with the aid of some „living" stones from the Red Sea and the Meditterranean, until the *Tetra Nitrite Jest Kit* read no more than 0.05 mg/l of nitrite nitrogen. Then, having established that my miniature reef was

'. fully opened colony of Dendronephyta divaricata, with blue damsel fish 'hrysiptera cyanea) and a Pseudochromis paccagnellae.

Photo: P. Wilkens

y for colonisation, I began to ire the species which I hoped d give the tank its special at- on. The first to move in was a ıy of magnificent yellow cup s *(Tubastrea aurea)* a species of e coral which occurs on reefs throughout the tropical Indian and Pacific Oceans. Two closely related species, *Tubastrea tenuilamellosa* and *Astrodies calycularis* are found in the Caribbean and on the shaded shores of the eastern Mediterranean respectively.

Stone corals thrive in strong water currents, so I attached the colonies almost vertically in my artificial reef wall at a point where the rotary pumps were producing a powerful water movement. The yellow cup corals have to be fed with all kinds of animal food as a substitute for plankton, and the polyps are quite capable of swallowing fully grown freshwater and marine shrimps *(Mysis),* and other similarly sized pieces of food. Frozen shrimps, mussel and squid meat are quite acceptable and can be fed in suitable small pieces, using forceps, after it has been allowed to soak in a little sea water. As each polyp is part of the same colonial organism it is not necessary to feed them all individually, and it is quite sufficient to feed four or five individuals each day.

Having successfully started off my new aquarium I then went on to acquire three different species of soft corals; the yellow-orange coloured *Dendronephyta aurea, a* large colony of red-white *Dendronephyta divaricata* and the beautiful deep orange-red *Carotaleyon sagamianum.* With their small polyps all these species can be more easily fed in the same way as the sh-allow water leather corals; *TetraTips* and various kinds of freeze-dried foods are crushed to a fine powder with a laboratory mortar and pessel, and the resulting mixture is suspended in a little sea water. Using a plexiglass tube this "soup" is introduced into the water just above the little animals, and by using a magnifying glass it is easy to watch their eight feathered tentacles reach out to trap the tiny particles of food. As with the stone corals these species also require a fairly strong water current, and in the-wild they only settle where there is a moderate to strong current or where a constant swell creates a vertical movement of the water.

Over the course of a few months the colourful soft corals developed into magnificient colonies and seemed to thrive on their diet of finely ground *TetraTips.* Indeed, as this powdered food does not break up immediately in the water but remains for some time as tiny grains, the leather corals could also be fed very successfully in this way. The carrot-like *Carotalcyon sagamianum* doubled in size within six months, and the red-white colony of *Dendronephyta divaricata* also developed splendidly. The individual branches sprouted tiny twigs, with at first one and then more and more secondary polyps. A second colony, which I rescued from a friend as they were not exactly thriving in his brightly illuminated tank, soon recovered in my special tank and put out new subsidiary polyps even on branches which were showing signs of previous degeneration. In the past I have noticed with the various light loving species, almost all of which accomodate symbiotic algae, that feeding vitaminised artifical plankton has a very

The soft coral Dendronephyta aurea thrives in strong water currents away from bright lights. *Photo: P. Wilkens*

beneficial effect on the maintenance of their brilliant colours. Hence, two or three times a week I soaked the dry food in a few drops of multivitamin solution before feeding the colonies.

One of the problems with using very finely ground food is that some of it inevitably gets lost in the tank, and to overcome this I added some tropical sand stars and small, non-predatory starfish, to clean up the remnants. Two sea cucumbers which vacuumed the ground and the rocks with their oral tentacles also proved to be ideal scavengers. However, as this method of feeding increases the biological loading of the water quite significantly compared with an aquarium containing only fish, care must be taken to provide the best possible protein skimming system. It is quite surprising to see how clear and clean the water remains if an efficient system is employed.

In addition to the stone corals and colourful soft corals I also keep two other representatives of the reef community, namely the horn corals and the sponges. The former I will not describe in detail here, except to say that they thrive and appear very hardy under the maintenance regime already mentioned. The sponges, however, include some of the most interesting forms of life found in the sea and I should like to say a little more about them.

These strange filter feeders have evolved a variety of shapes and that they have existed in the oceans, and are the most primitive of all the multicellular animals we endeavour to keep in our marine tanks. Unfortunately, though they often prove difficult to acclimate to the aquarium environment and many species,

Two sponges, Dasychalina spp. and Pseudsuberits spp., with a red starfish (Fromia millporella) and a blue crust sponge (Haliclona permollis), in the foreground.
Photo: P. Wilkens

particularly the most beautiful representatives, are renowned for being very sensitive and frail. However, with more and more invertebrates being imported from the subtropical seas, we are getting an increasing number of sponges which are not only hardy but also show a very rapid growth rate. Examples of such species are found in the genera *Haliclona, Halichondna* and *Clathria,* the blue, yellow orange and red crust sponges that inhabit the dim depths of coral reefs, and many of these thrive exceptionally well. The same applies to the various so called cork sponges of, for example, the *Tethya, Suberites* and *Pseudsuberites* genera, and last but not least the bath sponges, *Euspongia officinalis* and the horse sponge *Hippospongia communis.* These latter two have subspecies and strains throughout the warm seas of the world, and both thrive extremely well in a marine aquarium.

One of the most important points to remember when dealing with sponges is that they cannot tolerate exposure to air for more than a few minutes. Fortunately this has now been made clear to both the collectors and dealers, but the aquarist himself should take great care when putting them into the aquarium. Most species must be placed in a shady spot in the tank so that they do not become covered with algae, and many do better if kept in their own special tank with only dim lighting. Although there are numerous species, especially from the Caribbean (one of the world's richest "sponge grounds"), which are exposed to strong light and probably produce various substances to prevent algal growth, the aquarist is still well advised to place his specimens away from direct lighting. Like the soft corals, sponges also like plenty of water movements as it provides them with a supply of fine food particles, and at the same time prevents them becoming suffocated by inorganic debris which drops onto them.

Feeding sponges in the aquarium is not particularly difficult, and I do not feed mine very heavily as, judging by their surprisingly good growth, they seem to get enough food via the soft and horn corals. Various liquid and semiliquid prepared foods (which must be appropriately diluted), have proved highly satisfactory, and now and again I feed a little yeast suspended in sea water, or a few millilitres of a micro algae culture which can easily be grown on a window sill or balcony. Actually I tend to reserve the latter, rather special food for unknown species which look rather delicate, such as the *Dasychalina* species illustrated.

One problem that always occurs when sponges are kept in aquaria for long periods of time is that the originally brightly coloured animals gradually fade and lose their brilliance. It is known in the scientific field that carotenoids, although ba-

Sea cucumbers are relatives of the starfishes and sea urchins. The make good scavengers, although some forms are difficult to feed.

Photo: K.Paysan

sically of vegetable origin, are responsible for the colouring of innumerable animals, and experiments have been carried out to investigate the effects of artifically adding these compounds to the diet of sponges. Small quantities the principal colouring agent in ripe tomatoes and paprika, crocetin, the yellow pigment in saffron, and astaxanthin, the colouring substance in many marine and freshwater crabs, were added to the food given to various species and the results were remarkable!

Grey-white colonies of the crust sponge *Halichondria incrustans* turned a deep orange within a few weeks and the purple sponge *Lotrochata purpurea* which often fades to a pale pink also regained its vivid natural colouration.

Following the advice of Dr. Ritter, whom I knew in connection with his excellent work for *Tetra* in West Germany, I then tried feeding *Tetra Ruby,* and was pleasantly surprised by the results obtained after the flakes had been ground down to a fine powder. In particular my *Dasychalina* colony recovered its purple-brown colour, and a nearly white colony of *Lotrochota* sponges took only two weeks to resume their beautiful pale purple! Hence for some time I have been preparing the following „recipe" for my various sponges: a teaspoonful of finely ground *Tetra Ruby* is added to about a quarter pint of sea water in a flask, and, if available, some crushed water fleas, freshwater shrimps or other crustaceans are included as an additional source of carotenoids. After adding a few drops of a multivitamin supplement, this "paste" is shaken for 5-10 minutes, and is then introduced into the water around the sponges, via a piece of fine tubing. Using this feeding regime of commercially produced foods, plus yeast, micro-algae etc., I have not only been able to keep some magnificient sponges, but have also been able to breed them successfully. Some of my sponges now cover large areas of the shady parts of the tank, although it is unfortunate that their gorgeous colours are only truly revealed by the light of a torch!

There is no reason why fish cannot be kept in a special invertebrate tank, provided that only small species are selected. I currently have some blue damsel fish *(Abudefduf asimilis),* a *Pseudochromis paccagnellae,* two *Nemapteleotris magnificus* and two pair of *Synchiropus splendidus.* Feeding very fine fish foods also provides nutrients for many microorganisms and tiny creatures such as the crabs *Tisbe furcata* and *Microcalanus* spp., and amphipods and isopods which were introduced with the living stones, and which form a kind of food chain in the aquarium. Incidentally, omitting the use of a protein skimmer, even if possible, is not recommended since this really will prevent the inclusion of fish in the tank and will necessitate changing part of the water quite frequently. I hope that this article has shown that the fascinating creatures of the twilight coral reefs can be kept without lavish specialised facilities, and I would be delighted if I have stimulated just one or two of you to set up an invertebrate aquarium!

by Peter Wilkens

Sea slugs in the marine aquarium

At first glance it is difficult to imagine that the exotically beautiful sea slugs are even remotely related to the more familiar hard shelled snails. With their bizarre bodies and feathery outgrowths, they seem more like the product of an over vivid imagination! However, these unusual marine invertebrates are the products of natural selection which has carefully shaped them to suit their individual lifestyle, and today there are some 4500 species occurring throughout the word, from the cold waters off the American continent to the tropical Indian Ocean. They are found in shallow coastal waters and in the great depths of the open seas, thriving on muddy sea floors and on brightly lit coral reefs, in dense seaweed beds and wa[illegible] fields of eel-grass.

There are two types of sea slugs which are commonly available, both of which belong to the sub-class which have their gills at the rear of

Flabellinopsis iodenea from California. *Photo: H. Debelius/KAN*

A sea slug with its strip of eggs.

their bodies, the Opistobranchia. The first of these, the Pleurocoela, have covered gills and are represented by the sea hares (Aplysiidae). These animals are quite well known and can easily be kept in the aquarium. It is the second group, the naked gilled Nudibranchia, which I would like to concentrate on, and although I am not experienced enough to identify every species of slug individually, I would like to introduce some of these animals in the accompanying photographs.

As the reader may know, the identification of sea slugs cannot be based on their colouration alone, as many species throughout the 48 families change their appearance between the juvenile and adult stages. Accurate identification has to be based on examination of tentacle shape, the digestive organs and the structure of the kidney sac, none of which makes life any easier! My illustrations are therefore intended only to demonstrate the beauty of a number of animals that have not, as far as I know, been popularised in any other available publication. The photographs which show the natural habitat of the various species were taken by divers known to me personally, and the observations I have

Algal eating slugs of the family Glossodorididea.

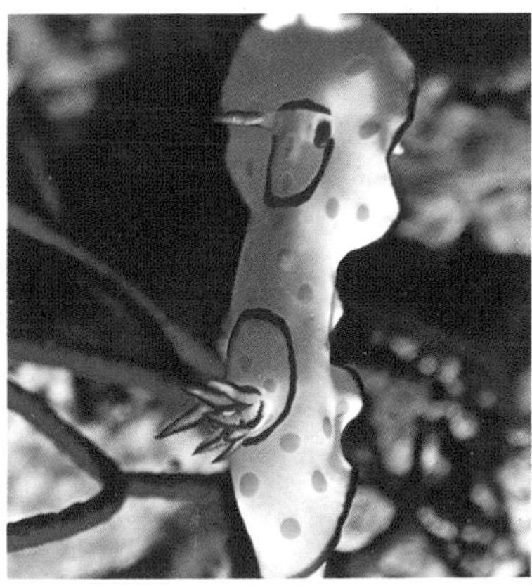

A slug from the sub-family Cadlininae.

A member of the family Chromodoridi-dea from the Indo-Pacific.

made from specimens in the aquarium do not appear to be paralleled in the current literature.

Hopefully this article will provide food for thought and stimulate further study of these fascinating creatures, as our current knowledge is somewhat limited.

The sea slugs have undergone a number of dramatic changes during their evolution, including the loss of their shell and mantle cavity which normally house the reproductive organs, rectum and gills. Breathing is now carried out through the skin or through external gills, which vary

The beautiful Tridachiella diomeda which lives in the Gulf of California.
Photo: W. Daum/IKAN

An unidentified species which feeds on sponges.
Photo: W. Daum/IKAN

in position and complexity. In all genera of the suborder Doridacea for example, they grow like a wreath of short feathers around the posterior anal opening, and can be withdrawn into a special cavity if the animal is threatened. The Doridacea also bear two large antenna-like olfactory organs at the anterior end, together with smaller tentacles which serve as tactile organs. None of these animals grow much longer than 2 ins and it is these species which are often available commercially. Unfortunately only the invertebrate enthusiast is likely to remember names such as *Glossodoris, Chromodoris, Archidoris* and *Peltodoris, as* there are hardly any common names for these slugs. In contrast to the small, creeping doridaceans, the closely related genus *Hexabranchus* includes species which grow up to 12 ins in length and are particularly good swimmers. They have broad flaps along the sides of their bodies which act as supports, and the foot forms itself into a tube from which water is expelled by contractions of the foot muscles. I have been par-

Chromodoris uadricolor on a horn sponge inthe Gulf of Agaba.
Photo: H.Debelius/IKAN

Another species showing the wide variety of colouration within the Chromodorididae.
Photo: W.Daum/IKAN

ticularly fascinated by the undulating, often erratic, movements of the bright red *Hexabranchus sanguinius* from the Red Sea, whose behaviour I have been able to observe on underwater films taken by friends of mine. Scientists have discovered that this slug actually plays host to a species of decapod *(Periclimenes imperator)* which lives in the slugs' large clusters of dorsal gills. This is clearly an instance of commensalism as the tiny crustacean feeds on the excrement of the slug and nibbles at the plankton growing on it's body. When the sea slug leaves the ground and swims above the reef it's passenger clings firmly to it's bushy gills to avoid being swept away.

This little decapod probably 'realises' that when close to it's host it is protected from being eaten by its natural enemies, but how is it that the conspicuously coloured slugs themselves are not attacked? Scientific studies have shown that predatory fish usually ignore sea slugs completely, and that if one is swallowed, is very quickly spat out again! The answer to the mystery is to be found in the nature of the food which some of these animals eat: their diet consist of jellyfish, colonies of hydrozoans, and sponges. The strong stings of the hydrozoans, which are normally avoided as food, have no effect on the slugs, and the powerful sting capsules are stored undigested in their intestinal appendages. When necessary the capsules can be voided, at which time

Nembrotha eliora beside a Tubastrea coral in the Gulf of California.
Photo: H. Debelius/IKAN

they explode so that the slug's attacker is stung and learns to look elsewhere for a meal! In the case of slugs which feed only on sponges and moss polyps, they produce an unpalatable defensive mucus which again deters predators. All sea slugs are hermaphrodite, and their gonads can produce both egg and sperm cells. Their reproductive organs are situated laterally towards the rear of the body, and they reproduce by fertilising each other, a process I have often been able to observe in the aquarium. Two individuals come to lie side by side so that their sexual organs are in close contact, and sperm is carefully exchanged. Two to three days later the eggs are laid while the slug creeps in a circle round a central point, so producing a strip of eggs which is anchored firmly to the substrate.

However, whenever any of my animals successfully spawned they invariably died no more than three days later, a fact which I have been unable to explain. Being employed by a tropical fish importer, a considerable number of slugs pass through my hands, and I decided to experiment with some Doridacea in

The beautiful red Hexabranchus sanguineus dances elegantly through the water.
Photo: W. Daum/IKAN

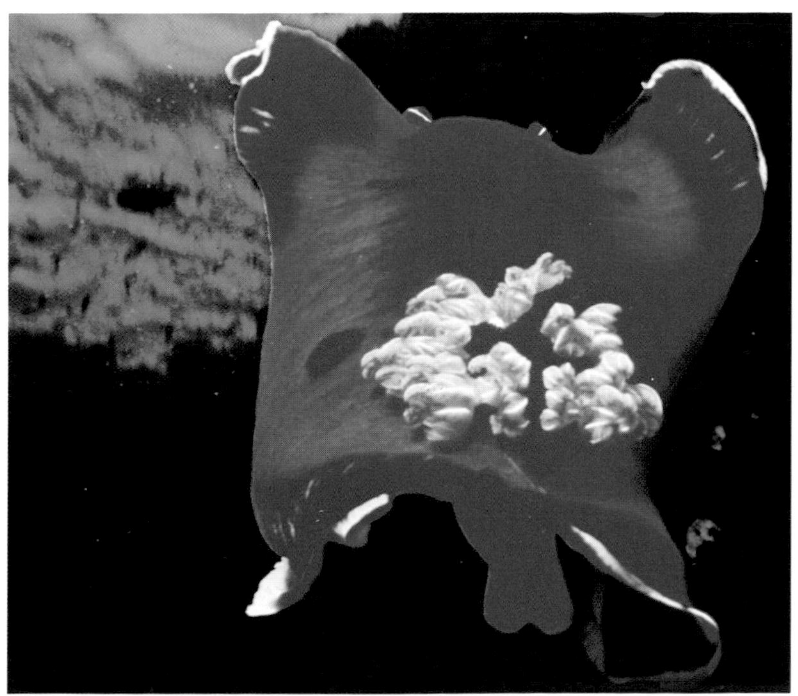

special tanks. When freshly imported they appear to be quite fit and also occasionally spawn, so after I realised that spawning resulted in their death I tried keeping them on their own. Unfortunately at first I did not know enough about feeding them, and they starved to death within a few weeks; however, after I saw some underwater photographs which showed the kind of sponges which Doridacea feed on, I managed to acquire some of them and subsequently kept one *Glossodoris* alive for almost twelve months.

Although my recent studies have been more encouraging, I am still not satisfied with the results, and as far as my work allows I shall continue to experiment, and I hope eventually to build up a much greater pool of information about keeping these magnificent animals.

by Wolfgang Daum

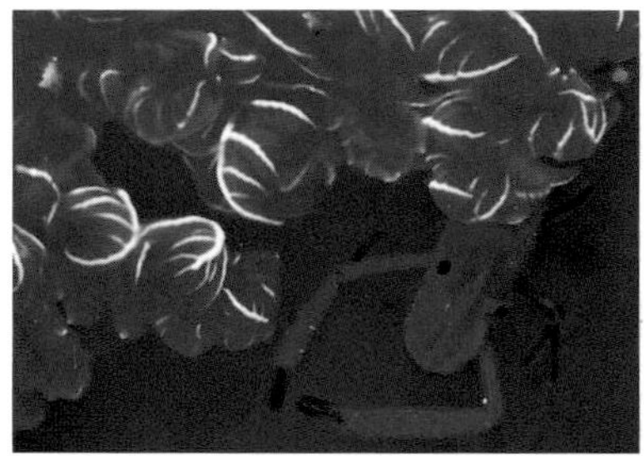

The decapod Periclimenes imperator which lives amongst the gills of H. sanguineus. Photo: W.Schott/IKAN

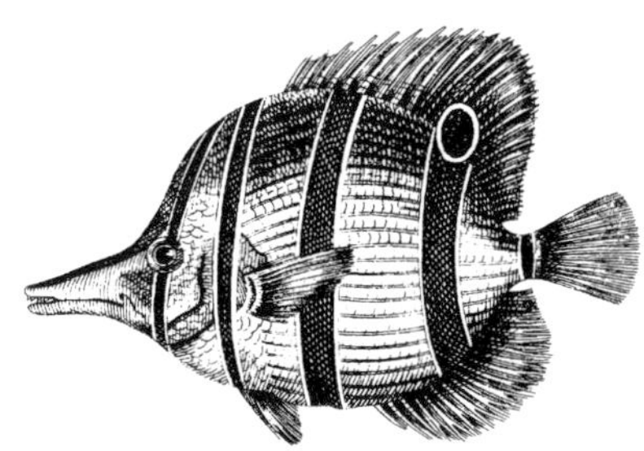

A snail pest of marine plants

Most plant life in the sea consists of various forms of marine algae. Of those suitable for the marine aquarium, the best known is *Caulerpa*, a green macro-alga. This group is common in various parts of the world, including the Atlantic and Indian Oceans, the Mediterranean and the Red Sea. *Caulerpa* is bright green in colour, and has the appearance of a higher plant. Different species do, however, have a great variety of shapes - from whorls of tiny grape-like forms to bushy, feathery leaflets. *Caulerpa* also has runners with root-like structures which attach it to the substrate.

In my marine aquarium (capacity 800 gallons), I have cultivated thirteen different species of *Caulerpa.* These algae grew so well that I frequently had to thin it out in the tank. However, much to my dismay, each of my *Caulerpa* species began to die, exhibiting no real symptoms. First the more fleshy species were attacked, although eventually none of the algae were safe. Red algae, in the same tank, remained unaffected. It was not for some time that I eventually realised the cause of the problem. Earlier I had noted that a small green snail had been introduced into the tank (perhaps with new marine plants or fish), and this did not only survive, but also actually reproduced. Being small, and well camouflaged, these snails built up to enormous numbers almost unnoticed. As a result their ravages on the *Caulerpa* were devastating. It seems that this snail (called *Berthelina chloris)* is quite frequently associated with *Caulerpa,* and is distributed over a wide range of marine locations. At certain times it's egg production can be very high, with numerous batches of spawn produced, each measuring 1/4-1/2 ins and containing 150-400 eggs. The gelatinous eggs hatch after about 7 days, liberating tiny larvae with a small shell. To aid in the dissemination of this otherwise slow moving mollusc, it makes use of the ocean currents to distribute it far and wide. Therefore, I hope that my experiences have been of some interest, and serve as a warning to other marine hobbyists. I for one will always quarantine all new marine plants for a week or so, away from my set-up tank, and examine them closely for signs of snails.

From an article by J. Birkholz

Berthelina cloris

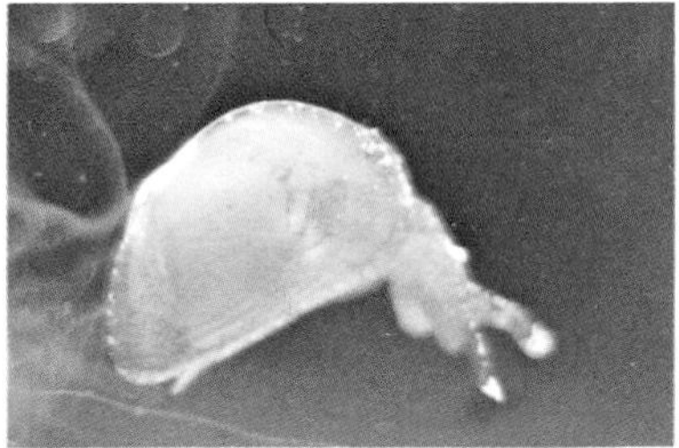

The coral reef tank at the Coral World in Eilat

Some five miles south of Eilat, on the Gulf of Aqaba, is located the Coral World of Eilat. This institute comprises a number of flat buildings housing a variety of installations such as a museum, fish tanks, kiosks, souvenir shops and the coral reef tank. However, there are also various other houses, like the underwater observatory, the shark tank, as well as the turtle and ray tank.

The 70000 gallon reef aquarium was put into service in May 1982, as the last part of the planned phase at that time. The original concept had allowed for a reef shelf section to accomodate mainly shoaling reef dwelling fish and some of the larger coral fish species. Primarily, the intention was to keep those types of fish that cannot be watched from the observatory or those that cannot be kept in the smaller aquaria because of their behaviour, lifestyle or size. The solid structure had to be formed in as natural a way as possible so as, to offer it's inhabitants a wealth of hiding places and - depending on the species - the opportunity to satisfy their behavioural requirements. The reef wall in the tank was made up of

A reef section with sessile coral branches and magnificently coloured coral fish.

A tubular sponge, Siphonochalina sp. The tubes serve a home or hiding place for many reef organisms.

The domed building at Coral World blend in with the landscape in a quiet harmonious way. Photo: H. Esterbauer

The crab, Scylarides tridacnofoides. *Photo: H. Esterbauer*

the skeletons of dead stone corals, of living, mainly stony corals, and of rocks and stones from the Gulf. This artificial reef was constructed as a circle with a diameter of 60 feet, 12 feet wide and 10 feet high.

Biologically sound water, still containing plankton organisms, is pumped from the sea from a depth of 12 feet. The water is first led into a sedimentation tank and thence into the aquarium. The sedimentation or storage tank serves on the one hand to hold back heavy marine sediments and on the other hand to maintain the water supply for a few hours in cases when the supply is interrupted. This is because even a 15 minute stoppage could wipe out every form of life in the coral tank. From the reef aquarium the water flows back into the sea - due to gravity - via the shark and turtle tanks. The hourly exchange of fresh seawater amounts to some 16000 gallons.

However, the introduction of unfiltered seawater also brings problems. It means that organisms harmful to the fish stock are brought in and, in stormy weather, cloudy water can impair the viewing conditions. This

Actinodiscus (false coral) and Zooanthus (colonial anemones - left) which will also thrive in the home aquarium.

A divers-eye view of a coral reef.

Barracuda (Sphyrena flavicauda) is a roving reef predator, that can only be kept in very large aquaria. *Photo: P. Wilkens*

situation can, on occasions, clearly be a source of annoyance to visitors, particularly those that are keen to take photographs. Because only the circular visitor room is covered, and the coral tank is open above, the natural sunlight can be exploited to the full. This is one of the fundamental requirements if the zooxanthellae - and with them the corals and anemones - are to thrive. Optimum fulfilment of the basic physical requirements such as light, warmth etc., together with the combination of dozens of living corals and the throughput of clean water, create a largely natural exhibit. This biological equilibrium is further supported by the composition of the fauna.

Surgeon fishes (Acanthuridae) act as algae grazers, and various species of sea urchins can break down the film of green algae that generally covers the overall structure. A variety of organisms like crabs, sea stars and gastropds (sea snails) in turn recycle the remnants of food or eat any dead animals. This enables to a large extent the setting up of a self supporting ecological system in the aquarium.

by Hans Esterbauer

A look at the world of coral gorgonians

If you have recently paid a visit to your marine dealer's shop you have no doubt been amazed at the increasing number of colourful branched corals which are currently available - very tempting specimens indeed! In this article I should like to introduce three representatives, all of which are ideally suited for keeping in a marine invertebrate aquarium. The branched or tree corals belong to the large sub-class of the eight-rayed anthozoans or 'flower animals' (Octocorallia). Also included in this sub-class are the order Alcyonaria (leather corals), Stolonifera (tube corals) and Pematularia (sea feathers). The sub-class Octocorallia comprises about 2500 species. The species which I should like to describe here all belong to the order Gorgonacea (gorgonid or branched

Anthoplexaura dimorpha.

The mother colony (A) of Psammogorgia arbuscula.

corals). The representatives of this order usually form tree-like structures with arms akin to branches which are flexible at the tips, or alternatively, fanshaped structures. To date about 1200 species from the order Gorgonaria are known, including the sea fans, sea plumes and sea whips. On the outside of a tree coral is a firm outer tissue stiffened by numerous scattered limestone particles. This 'rind' contains openings into which the polyps can retreat. But in the centre of the colony these particles are fused into a solid, hard axial core or skeleton of flexible horny material known as 'gorgonin' So the skeleton is not completely rigid with limestone as in, for instance, the stony corals and the less calcium there is deposited in the skeleton, the more flexible will be the animal's structure, rendering it all the more suitable for life in a body of ever moving water. A polyp is a very simple animal with a sac-like body, the interior acting like a stomach and opening to the outside via a mouth, which is surrounded by tentacles. A coral consists of many of these polyps growing close together and interconnected by corals which penetrate the whole colony.

The first representative of the gorgonians I should like to write about is *Anthoplexaura dimorpha.* It belongs to the family Plexauridae and is mainly imported from the Philippines, where it seems to occur in some abundance. This branched coral is bushlike in form but only slightly branched. The pale to deep red outer tissue is quite thick and from this arise snow-white polyps about two millimetres in size.

These branched corals are among the varieties which are particularly adept at freeing themselves of any floating and suspended materials resulting from algae which may be growing upon them. The polyps can blow themselves up by drawing in currents of water into their body cavities. After some time the water is pumped out again and the layer of outer rind contracts, causing a mucous skin containing the waste particles, to slough off in pieces.

The first *Anthoplexaura dimorpha* which I acquired some two years ago had, at the time of capture, been simply ripped off the substrate by the collectors. It had only a very small disc which had furthermore lost the greater part of its outer layer. I anchored the disc of this damaged coral to a limestone rock in such a way that the disc could no longer be seen. Furthermore I chose a position for it so that it benefitted fully from the current of an aerator.

I then waited to see what would happen. In the evening, whilst I was feeding it with a plankton substitute, consisting of various species of freeze-dried foods and finely ground tablet food *(eg TetraTips),* I was delighted to see a number of white polyps venturing out from their protective layer. The next morning I was presented with a magnificent sight. The red outer layer was covered with masses of white polyps which were swaying to and fro in the powerful current. I was now able to watch just how voraciously the coral devoured any food which drifted by. To my joy I could see that the tips of the coral that had been damaged in transit were once more covered by the red rindlike substance.

After a short time there were even polyps appearing out of this new rind layer. Unfortunately, my hope that the rind substance would regrow in the area around the foot or that the coral would attach itself to the rock, did not materialise.

Although the *Anthoplexaura dimorpha* was situated in a very well illuminated part of my aquarium, I could not detect any build up of algae. Nor, apparently, did the direct light appear to make any difference to the coral. The polyps presented themselves promptly every morning at feeding time and the whole coral remained on full display throughout the day.

Overall, I can conclude that *Anthoplexaura dimorpha* is a very straightforward aquarium subject. The one prerequisite - apart from good water quality, of course - is their need for a strong current as the polyps will not open otherwise. After all, on the coral reef these varieties are to be found in particularly turbulent areas, such as the steep walls of the outer reef or in the channels between small coral islands.

It is not very fussy regarding the illumination. With this branched coral there does not appear to be too great a danger from colonisation by algae. Feeding with plankton substitute proved to be a great success with this coral.

The second branched coral that I should like to present is *Psammogorgia arbuscula.* The range of this magnificent, red coloured coral stretches over the whole of the Gulf of California.

It is some time ago now when I first bought a specimen of this species from a dealer. The specimen in question looked very much the worse for wear at the time. The blackish-grey axial skeleton was visible through the living horny layer in numerous places. Before the animal was eventually transferred to my aquarium, it firstly had to be acclimated to the water conditions in the tank. It was then subjected to a rather major 'operation' Using a sharp pair of clippers, I first cut off some of the pieces of coral which had become exposed and detached in order to prevent invasion by algae. The extent of the damage was such that I had to prune off three branches, which meant that - apart from the mother colony there were only three rather small arms left, each about 2 ins long. I sited these in various localities around my aquarium.

The large mother colony, referred to as 'A' hereafter, was placed in a light filled position with a strong current. Two smaller colonies ('B' and 'C') were installed in shady places where there was little in the way of a current. I attached one further colony ('D') to a small stone with a nylon thread and placed it in a cave with a very strong level of water movement. This colony did not get any direct light. Over the course of the months to come I was able to observe the different reactions and progress of the four colonies.

In the subsequent period B and C only opened sporadically and mainly at times when I was performing various duties in the aquarium, and thereby inevitably causing a current, or, alternatively when they were being fed. Later on, coral C was ripped off by a sea urchin an disappeared amongst the rest of the aquarium decoration. Coral B opened less and less frequently and eventually one day remained completely closed. To begin with, colony A only opened at night time, but soon allowed itself to be persuaded to open during daylight hours too, in response to food. Its polyps even put in an appearance. After a certain period of time this coral changed its daily rhythm entirely and soon I was

Mopsella ellisi is one of the most beautiful of the branched corals.

able to watch its polyps in action throughout the day. The bare patches on the axial skeleton were soon covered with red material once more and small polyps developed there.
Unfortunately, I lost a part of this coral when I changed the bottom substrate on one occasion. In doing so, presumably the fine dirt found its way into the pores causing some pieces of the horny layer immediately to become detached.
Colony A was also very subject to algae colonisation. Time and again green thread algae were swept onto the coral by the current. These filaments became caught up in the mother colony and grew at a rapid pace there - thanks to the strong illumination. As a consequence, the mother colony had to be cleaned regularly with a small pair of pincers to prevent the polyps from becoming choked.
My best experience was with coral D. The polyps first showed themselves after two days. It was noticeable that they put in an appearance during the day time right from the start. After just six weeks the area around the cut had grown over with the red rind. After a further three weeks - the first polyp appeared there and there were signs of two new branches appearing.
After four months D was carried off by a sea urchin and a 2 mm wide ring around the axial skeleton was exposed. Using a thin nylon thread I attached the branch back onto a stone and put it back into the cave. Some two weeks later, the ring had grown over again and, what is more, a new branch was forming, much to my delight.
To summarise the above events, I would say that *Psammogorgia arbuscula is* best suited to a dark position in the aquarium where there is plenty of movement in the water. There are hardly any feeding problems. The best food to give is undoubtedly the plankton substitute already mentioned.
Surely one of the most beautiful of all branched corals is *Mopsella ellisi,* which is frequently imported from Sri Lanka and the Philippines. Its most noticeable feature is its pale to deep red outer, out of which peep relatively large, golden yellow polyps. This species is one of the most easily kept gorgonians.
When I obtained my first *Mopsella ellisi,* there was only a small piece of the disc visible out of the very thick outer layer surrounding is. I positioned it in the direct stream of an aerator in my aquarium, so that the branches bent visibly in the current. Because it had such large polyps I was able to feed it larger items of food, such as small water fleas which were taken avidly - as well as the usual plankton substitute. Like other branched corals it was fed once or twice a day. For feeding I usually brought the items right to the coral using a glass feeding tube.
With this excellent diet the injured spot on the coral's food healed rapidly. The disc also expanded so that

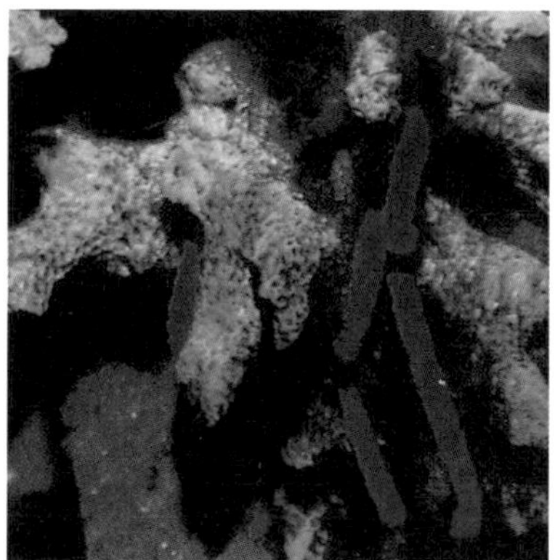

Offset (D) of P. arbuscula.

the whole animal was soon firmly anchored as part of the decoration of the tank. The ends of the individual branches soon started to grow too. Just like the species dealt with first, *Mopsella ellisi* does not seem to be especially sensitive to direct light. Perhaps this is due to the fact that, just like *Anthoplexaura dimorpha,* it has a self-activating cleaning mechanism at its disposal which it uses to rid itself of any dirt and accumulations of algae.

I have kept branched corals together with soft and leather corals, disc anemones as well as tube worms and stony corals. One thing to be sure of though, is to provide sufficient distance between the various species so that they do not sting each other and thus impair each other's development.

4 photos and text by D. Brockmann

Cespitularia, a soft coral from the family Xeniidae

It was as long ago as 1828 that Ehrenberg established the family of the Xeniidae, and since then (of course) the leather coral *Sarcophyton ehrenbergi* has been named in his honour. It is only over the last few years that representatives of this family, such as *Anthelia, Xenia, Sympodium* and *Cespitularia,* have been imported in increasing numbers for inclusion in marine aquaria, because their transport to and around North America and Europe posed a great deal of problems for a long time. Many of the soft corals of the family Xeniidae collapse shortly after they have been collected, even if they are loosened from the reef

Cespitularia from the Xeniidae.

with a piece of the original substrate attached. They also produce a lot of mucus, and consequently soon spoil the water in which they are being shipped. The xeniids do not possess any stinging cells and so this tendency to exude large amounts of mucus may be connected with some defence mechanism against competitors for living space on the reef. However, in the course of time it has become evident that these creatures need to be 'deslimed' thoroughly before they are transported around the world. To achieve this the exporter will agitate them again and again by touching them while they are still in his tanks, making them contract and give off a layer of mucus and, ultimately, to deslime them effectively. In addition, the native catchers have learnt to handle these animals with rather more care than was the case in the past. After all any specimens that perish in the tanks of exporters (and importers) represent a significant financial loss! In contrast to other, rather more tough, leather corals however, these corals will continue to be a major shipping risk for the importer concerned.

The home of the *Cespitularia* species is the tropical regions of the Indian and Pacific Oceans and the Red Sea, where whole colonies of this coral have colonised entire reefs. Here they form part of the typical fauna community of the 'sunlight zone' where the water is very shallow, and even in areas of light shade to depths of 10 to 40 feet.

Like all soft corals, *Cespitularia* also likes a moderate to strong current. This species is not fussy about the kind of substrate it chooses to colonise. As well as natural reef rocks and coarse coral sand, it will settle on mussel shells, macro-algae and even the glass sides of the aquarium. Asexual reproduction takes place via the lobular 'runners' that go out from the 'parent' The first growths of new secondary polyps form on the upper side of this runner when the 'lobe' has grown to about half an inch in length. If the runner finds a piece of substrate that appeals to it, it will start to grow there. The rear end of the lobe then constricts to a thin thread that continues to connect the offshoot to the 'parent' Very soon the secondary polyps start to shoot towards the light. Once these are large enough to capture the requisite amount of light on their own accord, the thread breaks and an independent animal comes into being. In a reef aquarium that is functioning properly this soft coral will often multiply itself quite readily. And a good thing too, because these corals can be swopped or given to other hobbyists as soon as possible, so as to protect the stock and avoid the need for any subsequent purchases at your local dealer. An important point to bear in mind once you have bought one of these corals, is to accustom it to its new aquarium conditions as carefully and slowly as possible. For this, the generally recognised drop method for adapting it to its new water surroundings has proved successful. If the newly acquired creatures are to thrive - and this applies to all light dependent invertebrates that have been kept under some other source of light at the dealers than the one we might have installed in our home aquarium - then they have to be acclimated quite slowly to the new light regime. This is particularly true of HQI (or metal halide) lamps, if the creatures are to be spared from possible light shock from which they will have difficulty in recovering, if indeed they recover at all. What may be one of the most effective forms of aquarium lighting for a reef aquarium stocked with inhabitants of the shallow water zone, is via *mercury* vapour lamps. However, *Cespitularia* soft corals can also be kept very successfully under fluorescent lamps. For an aquarium two feet wide and up to two feet deep, some 6 tubes of a range of different spectral qualities, including cool white and *Grolux,* should be used.

Unfortunately, fluorescent tubes do have a disadvantages, namely that the amount of UV radiation they produce is low. Anyone who has the facilities should conduct some experiments with the so-called ‘black light’ or ‘actinic’ tubes. These types of fluorescent tubes have a higher degree of UV radiation. But do be careful: these tubes must be operated separately by means of a time clock and perhaps not for longer than a few hours a day, and you should protect your eyes from these tubes too.

Like all Xeniidae, *Cespitularia* also possesses a much reduced coelenteron and cannot consume any particulate food. Presumably the soft coral takes in part of its nutriment via absorption of dissolved organic compounds. The main energy donors for *Cespitularia* are zooxanthellae, single celled algae that live in a very close symbiotic relationship with it. These symbiotic algae - which live in the endodermal layer of the coral - utilise the products of the coral’s metabolism, such as nitrogenous compounds and carbon dioxide, and supply oxygen in exchange. Similarly, nutrients in the form of simple protein compounds, amino acids, etc. are also supplied by the algal cells. So, in order to maintain its vital functions this soft coral needs its symbiotic relationship with the zooxanthellae. The system will only work where there is sufficient light and a good movement of the water to ensure that a supply of fresh nutrients is always to hand.

After carrying out observations with aquarist friends of mine I have ascertained that *Cespitularia* is only a long lived creature in water that is low in dissolved nutrients. The nitrate figure should be between 5 and 10 milligrams per litre.

Under no circumstances should it exceed the 10 mg/l limit. For this reason, a protein skimmer is re-

commended to reduce the amount of dissolved organic matter. Furthermore, a suitable denitrifying filtration system can also be installed in order to prevent a build up of nitrates, although regular partial, water changes with clean low nitrate salt water will achieve the same effect.
On purchasing these corals you should carry out a thorough examination to track down any parasites they may be carrying. These will generally be flat worms and tiny slugs that have adapted themselves incredibly well - both in form and in colouration - to their coral host. They should be removed immediately.

Text and photo by R *G. Rohleder*

Some less common soft corals

No other branch of the marine aquarium hobby has experienced such an amazing boom over recent years as the keeping of leather or soft corals. This is due on the one hand to the fact that the import of these creatures has been deliberately increased, and on the other to the fact that they are now being imported in such good condition that they can easily be acclimated to our aquaria without any great difficulty. The variety of species available has also increased considerably over the last few years. Whereas a few years ago most marine aquarists were only familiar with the *Sarcophyton, Lobophytum* and *Sinularia* species, nowadays they also keep and tend to prefer *Litophyton, Xenia* and *Anthelia* species. Another factor that plays a part in the advancing popularity is that in almost any large batch of imports from East Africa, Sri Lanka or Singapore, new species may be discovered.
The soft coral, *Litophyton arboreum,* from the Nephtheidae family, has been imported for some time now. This family is known to many marine hobbyists from the highly colourful and crepuscular *Dendronephtya* species which are encountered in all tropical seas on shady reef faces where there is a powerful current. The *Litophyton arboreum* described here, which is found throughout the whole of the Indo-

Australasian area, represents one of the few representatives of this family that provide a haven for symbiotic algae. For this reason the favourite colonisation area of this coral lies in quite modest water depths of no more than 30 feet or so.
The first imports of these soft corals proved to be delicate in the extreme. The reason for this was certainly to be found in the fact that the people who were catching the specimens of *Litophyton arboreum* were detaching the creatures from their substrate with a knife and shipping them off in this state. It is true that these eight rayed polyps did subsequently open up in the aquarium, but only a very few of them re-attached themselves to their new substrate.
Most of them started rotting at the point where they had been cut and became completely detached in the following weeks. And it did not seem to help at all if the stem was cut back with a sharp knife (as is possible with the *Sarcophyton* and *Sinularia* species), and the remaining portion of soft coral secured to a piece of rock with a nylon thread. Only in the rarest of cases was there any regrowth to be seen. Often the *Litophyton arboreum* would start to rot once more at precisely those places where the nylon thread was pressing into it and soon the soft coral was beyond hope. Fortunately, it soon became apparent that dealers were showing a degree of resistance to this kind of import which meant that only such soft corals were being sold that had at least a small piece of substrate attached. In this condition, imported *Litophyton arboreum* displayed far greater durability.
With the aid of this piece of substrate the creatures can now be incorporated very easily into the decoration. As has already been mentioned, because they harbour symbiotic algae they should always be kept in very light conditions. Illumination with metal halide lamps has brought excellent results. Where the illumination is sufficiently intense the growth rate to be seen *in Litophyton arboreum* is tremendous. Colonies that have been imported at a size of 3-4 ins frequently double their initial size within a year. Furthermore, this soft coral can be fed on a good quality plankton substitute.
Once an individual has settled down it proves to be remarkably tough and durable. Right from the start they display a marked daily rhythm. Shortly after the light goes on the little polyps of *Litophyton arboreum* open completely. Provided that they are not disturbed, they remain open all day long and only close when the light goes out.
This soft coral bears a very striking resemblance to the extremely dangerous, sharp stinging anemone *Actinodendrum plumosum.* Because of its marked propensity to inflicting stings, this anemone is hardly worth considering as a subject for keeping long term in the company of other invertebrates. Therefore, it is far

The soft coral Litophyton arboreum.

better to keep *Litophyton arboreum* in a community tank. Although they are amongst the soft corals with the strongest sting, you need have no qualms about putting them in with other invertebrates so long as a sufficiently wide safety margin is left between them and other sessile occupants of the aquarium.

Whilst the artificial propagation of some leather or soft corals scarcely presents problems any more, there are still considerable difficulties with *Litophyton arboreum.* Earlier on I mentioned that injured specimens very quickly start to rot and rapidly degenerate. Similar problems are encountered with artificial propagation. If one cuts off a branch to use as a cutting or side-shoot, then it can happen that both the parent *and* the offshoot start to rot and ultimately perish. Nevertheless, if you do want to try to raise a young specimen in this way, you should start with a really well established *Litophyton arboreum.* Moreover, the detached arm should be set into the decoration in such a way that it is not squashed if at all possible. In addition, the offset should be placed in a very light position, where there is a very powerful current. If these hints are followed, then it is possible to succeed with the occasional offcut from this species. Apart from this, once this soft coral is established it is not at all

fussy and it can be recommended to anyone who has had a little experience in the keeping of invertebrates. As far as fish are concerned, it can be kept with any species that is not by nature an attacker of this type of creature. However, after certain recent experiences I have had, some care is warranted if these are to be kept with surgeon fish of the *Acanthurus* genus. I should like to make specific reference here to the gold-rimmed surgeon, *Acanthurus japonicus.* In my aquarium this surgeon soon turned into something of a „wolf in sheep's clothing".
A short while ago I bought a *Litophyton arboreum* which, to my immense pleasure, developed very well indeed. Then, six months later, large quantities of thread algae started to develop in my aquarium and sol decided to put a surgeon fish into the tank to combat this menace. In the course of my next visit to a dealer's I duly bought the above mentioned specimen of *Acanthurus japonicus.*
Throughout the acclimation period I did not observe any attacks at all on any of the invertebrates and indeed these are said not to be expected from this surgeon fish. Yet one day I did notice on various Octocorallia, to which group *Litophyton arboreum* belongs, a number of isolated injuries to the ends of the branches. On closer inspection it appeared to me as if at the very tips the polyps, together with their tentacles, were missing. This condition was particularly alarming in the *Litophyton arboreum* and to such an extent that I feared that I would lose this magnificent specimen of soft coral.
Since the cause of the injury was not apparent to me, I decided to spend a long period of time in front of the aquarium over the next weekend in order to track down the source of the problem. However, I did not have to wait long. Shortly after the light over the aquarium went on, the surgeon fish emerged from its hideout, swam around the aquarium a few times and then commenced biting into the tips of the arms of the *Litophyton arboreum* and some of the other soft corals. But to my astonishment it did not eat the polyps but simply chewed them up and spat out the bits. Stone corals and the *Sarcophyton* species on the other hand were spared this treatment.
In order to avoid further injuries to these soft corals, I caught the surgeon fish and removed it from the tank. Once the *Acanthurus japonicus* was off the scene, the *Litophyton ar*boreum and the other soft corals very quickly recovered.
Of course, I cannot comment on whether these attacks are species specific or whether my *Acanthurus japonicus* was an exception to the general rule. Even so, in future I shall not be keeping this species of surgeon fish in my invertebrate aquarium.
The second species of soft coral that I should like to present here is very reminiscent of a tiny apple tree. This

Litophyton arboreum contains large numbers of symbiotic algae.

Soft corals often do well in aquaria, but still need proper care.

tree-like soft coral has, to some extent, completely different requirements from the *Litophyton arboreum* and so I shall deal with these in some detail below.

The soft coral itself has a really curious shape. On its 1-2 ins long stem there are just a few little branches out of which protrude the individual secondary polyps. However, these few branches are crammed together so densely that they can scarcely be distinguished from one another.

Whereas *Litophyton arboreum* has a pronounced daytime/night-time activity rhythm, this coral's behaviour is quite different, in that it is always completely open, even at night. Only the individual secondary polyps are retracted at irregular intervals back into the overall mass of the body.

Even after an exhaustive search of the copious volumes of literature I have accumulated over the years, I could not come up with either a description or an illustration of this species so that I was forced to resort to experimentation once again when trying to acclimate it to my tank. The dark brown colouring of this soft coral is already an indication of the large population of symbiotic algae. For this reason I decided to locate the stone with the two corals which had, incidentally, been obtained from an import from East Africa, in the lightest possible spot in my aquarium. Over the next couple of days both colonies were always completely open. But then the coral that was subjected to the strongest effects of the current started to show some abnormal behaviour. It buckled at the middle of the stem and laid the branches with the secondary polyps on to the rock. Once I noticed this, I decided to relocate the colonies. The rock was now placed in a position in which there was only a moderate current. Unfortunately, this measure was by now too late and the damaged coral was beyond hope. It rotted at the buckled spot and thereafter perished quite quickly. The second colony was probably not damaged at all because it remained completely open over the subsequent period.

This soft coral was fed on fine plankton substitute but I could never say with any degree of certainty whether the food was actually being taken. For this reason it was of the utmost importance to install it in the lightest possible spot so that it could draw its energy entirely from the products of metabolism of its symbiotic algae. The last soft coral that I should like to discuss is once again an extremely simple subject to care for. This creature, which has been frequently imported from the Indo-Pacific region of late, is one of the bushy growing species.

I had the greatest measure of success with them when I positioned them in a strong current. Furthermore, I was able to ascertain that this soft coral, in spite of its quite sizeable secondary polyps, did not accept any of the plankton substitute that was offered to it. It appears that with its weak sting it is not capable of holding on to the minute bits of food. As such, it belongs to that group of species that lives almost completely off their symbiotic partners. When kept in conditions that suit them, these corals display quite startling growth rates. In just four months the fingerlike appendages of the soft coral in my aquarium grew by about 1/2 inch. You can try to propagate this species without any great misgivings. To do this you just cut off one of the fingerlike projections with a sharp knife or a scalpel and fix it securely in the desired position in the tank decorations. Here it usually grows away quickly and is soon as big as the parent plant.

It is to be expected that more and more soft corals will be imported in the coming years and many of these will be hitherto unknown species. It would be a good thing if all the hobbyists who have had some meaningful experience with these creatures would publish their collective findings. In this way it might be possible to keep losses down to a minimum to the benefit of all our fellow aquarists and the animals we seek to keep.

Text and photographs
by Dieter Brockmann

Hydrozoans - to keep or not to keep?

Practically any item imported from tropical seas is likely to have the odd casual traveller on board, and these stand a chance of being a source of either delight or despair to the aquarium owner. One is often quite amazed at what actually turns up in the aquarium and especially what multiplies and thrives. I should like to give an account of such an animal in this article.

The creature in question is a hydrozoan polyp that I was given by a friend in the local club about a year ago. This polyp had already formed extensive colonies in its previous tank, so that my associate had no qualms about detaching a piece of rock that had been colonised by it. This hydroid probably belongs to the order Athecata, possibly to the genus *Tubularia.* I cannot be precise about this because I do not have adequate reference books. The individual brown polyps grow to a height of some 1/2 ins, arising out of a similarly coloured, branching mat of thin threadlike tissue. The diameter of the tentacles is about 1/8th inch. The creature is able to invert its crown and the upper stem section into a lower stem section, much in the way that the *Tubipora* organ corals do.

As this hydroid does particularly well in the lightest spots in my reef aquarium, I conclude that the species requires a lot of light. Closer observations then revealed that the species in question is one that is purely autotrophic (that is to say, one that is capable of sustaining itself solely on the metabolic processes ol their symbiotic algal partners).

Hydrozoans are hardy invertebrates for the marine aquarium. *Photo: P. G. Rohleder*

Evidence of this is provided by its behaviour in the aquarium. I have never yet been able to witness any sign of its accepting any food whenever I have offered it a plankton substitute. Quite the contrary in fact, because whenever any pieces of food touched it, it reacted by retracting its crown.

Reproduction or propagation takes place by a process whereby the parent polyp puts out a netlike system of lateral tubes (these are known as stolons) along the bottom, side panes, on the stems of leather or soft corals, or anywhere else for that matter - out of which fresh polyps burst. The stolons are also capable of standing up on their own and forming stems out of which the polyps will shoot. Ramose (branching) colonies will form in instances where the stem of the parent polyp splits. Furthermore, this species has the ability to send out individual polyps with a stem about 1/2 inch long out of the lower part of its base, and these then take root on any suitable substrate and in turn form further colonies. Thanks to the water circulation in the tank, these creatures have the capability for setting up colonies in any well lit area that might otherwise prove inaccessible. The hydroids also have the capacity to release free swimming, jellyfish-like sexual specimens, so called "hydromedusae" which are rather difficult to distinguish from genuine jellyfish. In aquaria reproduction is usually by asexual means (through the formation of runners or shoots, or through the production of individual polyps), as the separated medusae are likely to be treated as welcome additions to the diet by many of the other inhabitants of the tank, or will fall foul of the filtration equipment before they can mature.

It states in the literature that the tentacles are armed with a number of unusually large stinging cells. My observations seem to indicate that their stinging capacity is not all that great, because neither disc anemones, leather or soft corals such as *Xenia, Anthelia* (or similar creatures) that are subjected to direct contact from the polyps show any signs of ill effects at all. Nor are the hydroids damaged by the above mentioned creatures.

Looked at from this standpoint, these creatures represent ideal aquarium subjects if one disregards the possible disadvantage of their very high reproductive rate. In order to prevent them overwhelming and endangering other sessile subjects it is essential to thin out the hydroids regularly. This is best done with tweezers. Since in my experience hydroids do not inflict any damage, they should be regarded as an acceptable inmate in a well run, properly functioning invertebrate aquarium. It is even said that they are eaten by a number of specialist feeders like the dragonet *(Synchiropus),* though I cannot confirm this fact.

I would like to recommend that any owner of a tropical marine aquarium occupied by creatures from the shallow water zone should look around the tanks at his local dealers to locate some of these animals. If the water conditions and light levels are right there will be scarcely any problems to be encountered, because they are really quite hardy. Once these creatures have been introduced to an aquarium it will be hard to get rid of them again. Hydroids prefer a moderate water current and suitable illumination can be provided by metal halide lamps or daylight fluorescent tubes. A regular 10 % water change every month is, of course, essential.

Any marine aquarium owner who is interested in invertebrates will understand my penchant for sitting for lengthy spells in front of my reef tank watching these delicate and decorative creatures. For me, the notion of keeping invertebrates is the fulfillment of a long cherished dream since I first saw them in the aquarium of one of my friends. If you can take just a little trouble you will soon establish a 'living aquarium' in your home, that will thrive and grow. I hope that I shall be able to keep these magnificent, beautiful creatures for a long time to come.

by P.G. Rohleder

Linckia and Fromia - Two starfish for the reef aquarium

The sea stars or starfish all come under the class Asteroidea. The marine aquarist can choose from a huge range of species with diverse shapes and colours. Most of these stars are very straightforward to keep, though there are amongst them just a few specialist feeders. However, there is also something of a question mark as to whether all starfish can be kept in a community tank together with invertebrates. For our purposes the answer to this must be a clear 'no' since many of the stars are quite predatory by nature and would make a meal of any invertebrates they were invited to share a tank with. Those stars that have rounded arms are rather less predatory, or indeed not at all so inclined. Amongst these are the frequently imported blue *Linckia laevigata* and those species belonging to the *Fromia* genus.

The *Linckia* genus belongs to the order of the large disc-type sea stars which live in the tropical areas of all oceans. It possesses cylindrical, roller shaped, arms and is brightly, even garishly coloured. In rock pools and among drifts of seaweed specimens may be found that are completely light blue, voilet or burgundy in colour, with others being covered with dotted markings in contrasting poster colours on a plain background shade. They are harmless, durable creatures that lend themselves splendidly to the conditions offered by a reef aquarium. Their feeding requirements are simple for they eat the tiniest of animals in the food chain and detritus which is generally present in adequate amounts in a well established aquarium (say 2 to 3 years old). They can even be fed on *TetraTips* food tablets.

Linckia species display a remarkable capacity for regenerating themselves. Even a piece of an arm less than an inch in length can regrow into a complete starfish whereas in other species at least a piece of the body disc and a complete arm are necessary for this. These creatures also simply cast off an arm for purposes of asexual reproduction. On this there will soon develop four other little arms and after a certain amount of time a completely new sea star is fully formed. A replacement arm also grows to fill the gap.

The *Fromia* genus - which is mainly coloured various shades of red and often armed with fine, delicate black spines on the upper side of its body - can be recommended as being suitable for an aquarium with sessile (ie sedentary) occupants. There are three species that are imported to a greater or lesser degree from the Indo-Pacific area on a regular basis. These are:

- *Fromia milleporella* with a diameter of up to 3 ins;
- *Fromia manilis* up to 4 ins, and
- *Fromia elegans* which goes up to 3 ins in size.

These starfish do not need to be given any specific food because they will scavenge enough for themselves if the other inhabitants of the tank are fed regularly on a plankton substitute.

The *Fromia* and *Linckia* species will prove to be just as lively in their aquarium home as in theire natural habitat, provided that uninjured specimens are obtained and no air has got into their vessels and body tissue. Time and again the same mistake is made with these echinoderms of taking them out of the water when they are being caught and thus exposing them to air which is fatal for them, instead of transferring them from one place to another with the aid of a small plastic container. Obviously, it is impossible to know with any certainty whether they were removed from the water when they were captured originally and as such it is always a matter of conjecture as to whether they are indeed healthy. Nor is it apparent from their appearance. So what are the criteria on which a decision can be based when acquiring these animals?

There are just a few signs that the hobbyist should look out for. They should have a rigidly taut body. The specimens should not be bought if they have damaged arms, or arms with white specks on the skin. The tips of the arms should be examined thoroughly because it is here that tissue decay usually starts in cases where a bacterial disease is present. If you grasp one of these sea stars under water, they must close their mouth and retract their tiny tube or ambulacral feet.

A sea star from the genus Fromia.

The number of enemies that *Linckia* and *Fromia* have is not all that great. Smaller specimens and juveniles are occasionally regarded as fair game by certain predatory sea stars. Some snails, such as *Triton,* can even make a meal of fully grown specimens. However, the main predator of sea stars (apart, of course, from man) is the harlequin shrimp which feeds exclusively on starfish. Sometimes the *Linckia* starfish also hosts little parasitic snails *(Thyca ectoconcha)* in its arms where they will bore their way into the skin.

For obtaining food the *Fromia* and *Linckia* - as so-called 'grazers' - they move over the aquarium bed systematically searching for minute organisms that can be sucked in via the everted stomach. This capacity for everting the stomach and processing the food outside the body can be regarded as an unusual phenomenon amongst the invertebrate animals.

Their internal water tube system (or ambulacrum) distinguishes the sea stars from all other forms of life - except for creatures that are also classified within the echinoderms (Echinodermata), which includes the feather stars, the brittle stars, sea urchins and sea cucumbers (also known as sea slugs). This ambulacrum functions like a pumping system that conveys seawater throughout the insides of the starfish. The task of this unique system is to supply the animals with oxygen, to assist in the processing of the food and to act as a means of locomotion. The water enters via a sieve-like, perforated plate or disc, then flows through a channel with calcified walls to a ring channel that encloses the oesophagus. Leading off from here are five radial channels that in turn branch out into a multitude of little side channels. At the end of these there is a small vesicle and under each of these a small suction pad. The muscular interaction between the vesicle and the suction pad brought about by the pumping mechanism is what enables the animals to move about.

The nervous system displays the same ray-like symmetry. The mouth is surrounded by a ring of nerves, branching out from which there are five peripheral nerves. The majority of the sensory cells which are distributed over the entire upper surface of the body, are not highly developed. They react to visual, chemical and mechanical stimuli that they relay to a dense network of nerves lying just below the skin. At the very tip of each of these arms lies a special little foot. It is by means of this organ that the creature feels its way over its immediate surroundings.

Right above this organ there is an optic cushion, and also an accumulation of cells that acts as an olfactory organ. Some scientists are of the opinion that in their search for food starfish scarcely rely at all on their senses of touch and sight, but rather on a chemical sensing technique that combines the capacity for smelling and tasting.

The skin of the asteroids consists of three layers. There is a very thin layer covering the whole of its surface, including any bumps, small bristles and other protrusions. The sensory cells are embedded in this skin layer as well as glands in almost all cases and very often this layer has fine lashes or bristles. The purpose of these bristles is to keep away sand and other minute foreign bodies.

Under the epidermis of these animals there is a thicker hypodermis made up of connective tissue; it is in this layer that one finds the calcite skeleton, consisting of a series of regularly arranged calcium plates. This framework of plates varying in size and loosely joined together, helps to support and form the body.

The third layer of skin is as thin as the first. It is a type of peritoneum covering all the internal organs and lining the entire body cavity.

The sexual organs of the almost always unisexual sea stars lie between the arms as cluster-like sacs, and when the time for reproductive activity approaches extend well into the arms.

In the course of each reproductive cycle the females simply release into the open water the staggering figure of from two to more than one hundred million eggs - with the males following the procedure with their sperm. Out of these eggs hatch larvae that are initially extremely minute and these drift around in the water until reaching their final development stage.

To the layman the anatomy of an asteroid must seem very confusing.

Where is the front and the rear, the top and the bottom? You cannot make out a distinguishable head or tail. The 'front' is where a few dozen suction pads stretch out on any one of the arms to act as a trailblazer in a given direction in which it then sets off with an irregular stride and gait. I

by P. G. Rohleder

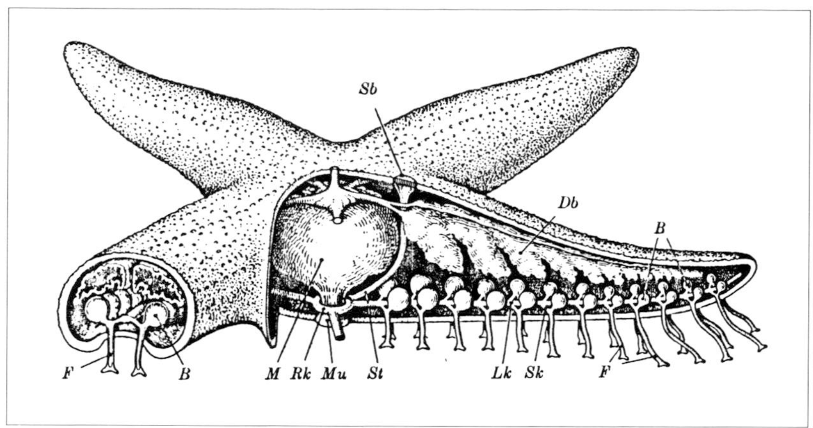

Structure of starfish

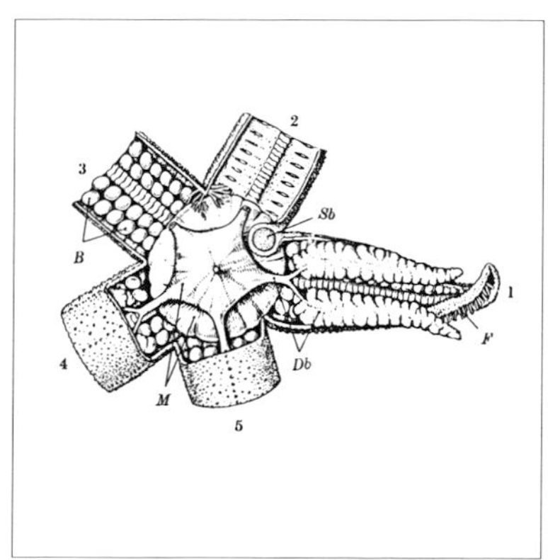

Structure from above

Legend to the Structure of the Sea Star:

Sb = Perforated plate
M = Stomach
St = Stone channel
F = Suction pads
Mu = Mouth
Lk = Longitudinal channel
B = Vesicle
Rk = Ring channel
Db = Intestinal bag

(Drawings were taken from the book 'Schmeil Tierkunde II', published by Quelle und Meyer Verlag, Heidelberg.)

And finally: Seawater for the aquarium

The most obvious difference between seawater and fresh water is in salt content. In most of the seas and oceans around the world the salt content remains relatively constant at about 35 grams per liter. However, there are exceptions. The Red Sea, for example, contains about 40 grams of salt for every liter of water; the North Sea has approximately 33 grams per liter; and the salt content of the Baltic varies between 5 and 25 grams per liter.
The salt content in seawater is produced by positively charged ions, known as cations, and negatively charged ions, known as anions, which result when certain chemical substances dissolve in the water. In an average sample of seawater with a salt content of 35 grams per liter, the following ions are present:

As the chart indicates most of the salt content in seawater comes from dissolved sodium chloride (NaCI), otherwise known as table salt.
The particular balance between positive ions and negative ions is very important in determining the pH - the acidity or alkalanity - of seawater. The surplus of anions over cations in normal seawater sets up a buffer system which tends to stabilize marine pH at around 8.2-8.4. Depending on the quantity of seawater involved, this buffer system permits a certain amount of acid or base to be added without changing the pH to any significant degree.
The salt content of the water is of particular value to the marine hobbyist in its relation to water density, also called specific gravity. Generally, the lower the salt content, the

Cations	Grams per liter	Anions	Grams per liter
Sodium	1 0.752	Chloride	1 9.345
Magnesium	1 .295	Sulphate	2.701
Calcium	0.41 6	Bicarbonate	0.1 45
Potassium	0.390	Bromide	0.066
Strontium	0.01 3	Boric Acid	0.027
		Fluoride	0.001

lower the specific gravity. Pure water which contains no salt has a specific gravity of 1.000 at 4 °C (39 °F); but in seawater with a salt content of 35 grams per liter, the specific gravity is 1.0278 at 4 °C (39 °F). Temperature is another factor which affects water density. As water becomes warmer, the specific gravity decreases. For example, the sample of seawater that has a specific gravity of 1.0278 at 4 °C (39 °F) has a specific gravity of 1.0234 at 25 °C (77 °F).

The table below shows the relation between salt content, density, and' temperature.

Controlling the factors of density, temperature, and salt content is of vital importance in a marine aquarium. Evaporation and other natural processes can result in drastic changes in the salt content of the water. These variations exert a powerful effect on the biological activities of fishes and can lead to illness and death.

by H. Leitz

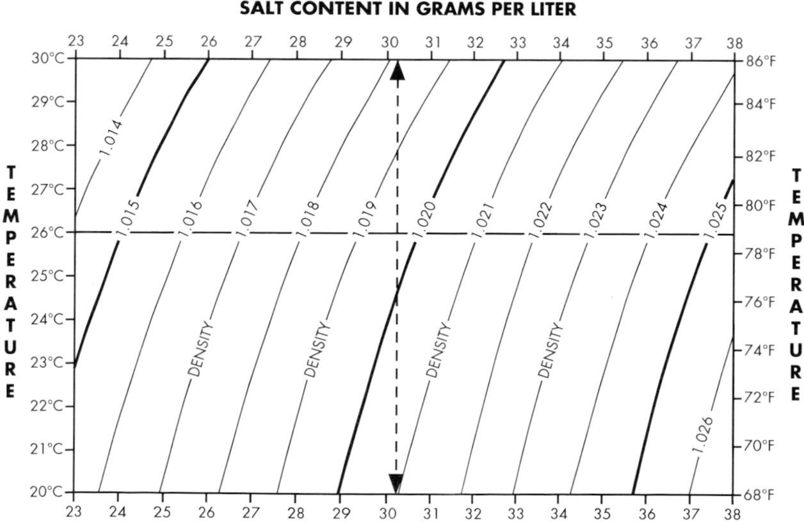

(NB. To convert litres to U.S.gallons, divide by 4.)

About the Author

Dr Chris Andrews is well known to fish hobbyists around the world. He is a regular contributor to TV and radio programmes, as well as hobbyist magazines, and has written several books. A specialist in fish diseases and fish breeding, he was Curator of the Aquarium, Reptile House and Insect House at London Zoo, but he now is working at the National Aquarium in Baltimore/USA.